PATRONS POVERTY & PROFIT
ORGANISED CHARITY IN NINETEENTH-CENTURY DUNDEE

Sir David Baxter

Patrons Poverty & Profit

Organised Charity in Nineteenth-Century Dundee

Lorraine Walsh

ABERTAY
HISTORICAL
SOCIETY

NUMBER 39
DUNDEE
2000

Acknowledgements

This project originated from research undertaken for my PhD thesis. Since the completion of that piece of work I have continued to look into the world of the charitable men and women of nineteenth-century Dundee and have never failed to be surprised and intrigued by what I find. I am grateful to Dr Jan Merchant, Honorary Editor of the Abertay Historical Society, for suggesting this project and to all the staff of Dundee University Archives, Dundee Local Studies Library and Dundee Archive and Record Centre for their help over the years. Thanks are also due to Mr Chris Davey, former Honorary Editor of the Society for his interest in my work, and last but not least, to my husband Kevin for his help and support.

Lorraine Walsh

January 2000

Contents

Introduction

Succour and Sentiment

'Amidst the anxieties of business, the excitement of money getting, and the numerous cares which the possession of wealth imposes, the townspeople do not neglect the duty of succouring the sick and the destitute, the widow and the orphan, the homeless and the friendless.'[1]

The history of organised charitable activity in nineteenth-century Dundee has hitherto been limited to brief references in general texts. These studies have concentrated largely on the history of the town's textile industry supplemented with revelations, often complete with salacious detail, about the social evils experienced in the town.[2] This rather narrow preoccupation with industrial production and poor living conditions has led to the development of a fixed image of nineteenth-century Dundee as a predominantly working man's - or rather woman's - town. To accept this picture without further question would be to do a disservice to the middle-class men and women of Dundee whose enthusiasm, time, energy - and of course money - went into the development of organised charity in the town.

During the course of the nineteenth century Dundee went through a process of dramatic social and economic change, experiencing the results of rapid population growth, economic development and changes in social structure, in common with the three other major Scottish towns of the period. Yet in many ways the experience of Dundee was distinct and unique. An increasing reliance on a single industry, textile - and specifically jute - manufacture, led to restricted employment opportunities in the town and a predominance of female workers. While the men, or 'kettle bilers', remained at home or in the public house, women workers in Dundee created a strong and vital workplace community which was seen as setting them apart from women workers elsewhere. Neither did Dundee have a counterbalance to her industry in the form of a collegiate culture, as did Glasgow, Edinburgh and Aberdeen. While their Universities were amongst the earliest academic foundations in Britain, Dundee did not see a seat of higher learning established in the town until the charitable foundation of University College in 1881, with the present University created only in 1967.[3]

Such factors had an impact on the development of Dundee as a distinct and unique society. The establishment of organised charities in the town was part of that individual experience, all the more so because their development was dependent upon the enthusiasm, determination and perseverance of middle-class Dundonians. Yet the Dundee middle class comprised a relatively small proportion of the population.[4] The individuals themselves, whose personalities and ambitions brought so much to bear on their level of civic and charitable involvement, further compounded this variable.

The growing wealth and personal status of the merchants and manufacturers in nineteenth-century Dundee created opportunities for their participation in the fashionable activity of philanthropy. As the century advanced it became clear that the new urban bourgeoisie were increasingly replacing the philanthropic role of the old charitable patrons, the landed families of the town and district. This situation was further intensified by the dominance of the textile industry and the occupational structure of the mills and factories where large numbers of individuals, and often many members of the same family, were employed by one manufacturer. This close association of employer and employee was open to the development of new urban forms of paternalism.

With a traditional system of poor relief based largely on the principle of voluntary contributions collected and distributed through the medium of the Kirk, almsgiving and individual acts of philanthropy were long established in the Scottish way of life. The first statistical account of Dundee (1793), noted that:

> The people of Dundee are inferior to none in generous exertions
> and contributions, either for the relief of particular distresses
> and misfortunes, or for the establishment and maintenance of
> public beneficent institutions.[5]

Others, however, had a very different perspective on the benevolence of Dundonians. The noted clergyman R.M. McCheyne's first impression of Dundee in the 1830s was of 'A city given to…hardness of heart'.[6] Indeed, despite the boasts made on behalf of Dundee's charitable residents, relatively few organised charities were actually established in the town over the course of the nineteenth century. Many charitable institutions found in the other major Scottish towns, such as a lying-in or maternity hospital, a Magdalene asylum (which aimed to reform 'fallen' women) and a Lock hospital (which treated individuals suffering from venereal disease), were notably absent from Dundee.

Moreover, the managers of those charities, which did exist often, encountered apathy, prejudice and resentment. The Orphan Institution, for example, was far from universally accepted by the Dundee townspeople. In the years following its opening the managers of the Institution regarded any criticism directed towards the charity as a direct reflection of the parsimony of the people of Dundee. They commented in 1816 that some 'may censure, where they only wish to excuse themselves from parting with their money', and that:

> Some, may be the almoners of other charities; who consider
> their trust as a sort of trading concern, and the public liberality
> as a fund which none but themselves should draw upon.[7]

By the annual report of the following year it was noted that whereas previously there had been 'many popular prejudices...afloat against the Institution' they had now died away. It was considered that while there may have been some individual bad feeling 'the tide of public opinion' had long since turned and had even begun to flow in the Institution's favour.[8] However, it is evident that animosity did continue towards the Orphan Institution. Only three years later it was felt necessary to minute a resolution 'to remove from the minds of the public, the unfavourable impressions which have of late been created against the Institution'.[9]

The Dundee Infirmary also attracted adverse criticism, even prior to its opening. The committee responded by asserting that the Infirmary was 'sufficient in every respect and that whatever reports to the contrary may have been circulated must have arisen from malice or ignorance'.[10] As for many other charities in Dundee, the townspeople appeared willing to support their initial establishment but proved less willing to support them in the longer term. For example, the 1831 Annual Report of the Infant Schools Society stressed that although it was 'probable that there are some who may entertain the expectation, that Infant Schools, when established, should support themselves...a small Annual Subscription' was still necessary to meet the expenses of the charity, including the salaries of the teachers.[11] The report of the following year made much of the unsolicited donation of four guineas that had been received from the town's magistrates.[12]

Philanthropic organisations could not survive without people who were willing to contribute both financially and in terms of personal time and commitment to the charities' support. An unwillingness to participate or the actual generation of animosity towards charitable organisations indicated that some Dundonians were reluctant to contribute to what was essentially the support of the town, in terms of both poor relief and moral guidance. It also indicated that prospective contributors were perhaps unhappy with the direction and focus of the charities. In order to access, and assess, the charitable nature or otherwise of nineteenth-century Dundee we must identify the contributors, the level of their participation in the town's charities, and examine the wider implications which their support of charitable organisations had for the town as a whole.

Notes

[1] Dundee Archive and Records Centre [DARC], GD/X207/1, *Handbook to the Charitable Institutions of Dundee* (n.d.).

[2] See for example, C.A. Whatley, D.B. Swinfen and A.M. Smith, *The Life and Times of Dundee* (Dundee, 1993); B. Lenman, C. Lythe and E. Gauldie, *Dundee and its Textile Industry 1850-1914* (Dundee, 1969) and W.M. Walker, *Juteopolis: Dundee and its Textile Workers 1885-1923* (Edinburgh, 1979). Lord Cockburn's comment, that mid nineteenth-century Dundee was a 'sink of atrocity, which no moral flushing seems capable of cleansing', is regularly quoted. See for example, C.A. Whatley (ed.), *The Remaking of Juteopolis* (Dundee, 1992), 12.

[3] M. Schafe, *University Education in Dundee 1881-1981* (Dundee, 1982).

[4] Stana Nenadic, 'The Rise of the Urban Middle Classes' in T.M. Devine and R. Mitchison (eds.), *People and Society in Scotland, Vol. I, 1760-1830* (Edinburgh, 1994); N. Morgan and R.H. Trainor, 'The Dominant Classes', in W. Hamish Fraser and R.J. Morris (eds.), *People and Society in Scotland, Vol. II, 1830-1914* (Edinburgh, 1995).

[5] *Dundee in 1793 and 1833: the First and Second Statistical Accounts* (St Andrews, 1991), 46.

[6] Rev. A.A. Bonar, *Memoir and Remains of the Rev. R.M. McCheyne* (c. 1892), 65.

[7] Local Studies Library [LS], Pamphlets D4485, Dundee Royal Orphan Institution [DROI], *Annual Report* (1816). It should be noted that the Orphan Institution, along with the Infirmary and the Asylum did not receive 'Royal' status until several years after their initial date of foundation.

[8] LS, Pamphlets D4485, DROI, *Annual Report* (1817).

[9] DARC, GD/AY/7/1/1, DROI, Minute Book, 1815-23, 23 March 1820.

[10] St Andrew's University Archives [StAUA], M415, Dundee Royal Infirmary [DRI], Minute Book, Vol. 1, 11 August 1794.

[11] LS, Lamb Collection [L.Coll.], 213 9A, *Report of the Committee of the Dundee Infant School* (1831).

[12] LS, L.Coll. 213 (9A), *Report of the Dundee Infant School* (1832).

Chapter 2

A Charitable Town?

'Perhaps there is not a town in Scotland the various direct charities of which give a better index of the benevolence of the citizens than Dundee.'[1]

One of the most remarkable periods in the history of charitable activity in Scotland, and indeed Britain as a whole, was the terrific upsurge in organised philanthropy which occurred from the late eighteenth century and continued throughout the nineteenth century. Although not new, the role of the subscription charity was revitalised in this period. In Dundee this was reflected in the emergence and development of both the large institutional organisations, such as the Infirmary and the Lunatic Asylum, as well as the various smaller societies which aimed to deal with the old and the sick, and the young and the orphaned of the town and district.

The incidence of organised charitable foundation in Dundee was somewhat sporadic and the overall number of charities established in the town before 1850 was relatively small. While Glasgow, Edinburgh and Aberdeen could boast a wide range of charities founded before 1820, many of which had eighteenth-century origins, Dundee had only a handful.[2] There was a resurgence of activity in the town from the mid to late 1830s, however, followed by a more intense period of charitable foundation after 1845. This period witnessed the re-establishment of some of the older charities, such as the Infirmary and the Lunatic Asylum, in new and enlarged premises. Charitable organisations with a medical focus were among the first to be established in Dundee, namely the Dispensary, the Society for Relief of the Indigent Sick, the Infirmary and the Lunatic Asylum.

A Dispensary had opened in the town in 1782, which by 1799 was treating in the region of 700 patients per year.[3] However, this did not stop other efforts being made with regard to the welfare of the sick poor. The Society for Relief of the Indigent Sick was founded in 1797 through the efforts of 'a few humane and benevolent persons in Dundee'.[4] Those involved in the new charity were careful to emphasise the particular circumstances of sickness and disease which created a distinct and exceptional situation necessitating charitable assistance. The Society noted that:

> In ordinary times...the people of this country neither expect nor
> desire the assistance of others - and this independent spirit
> cannot be too carefully encouraged.[5]

However, sickness or disease rendered them 'proper objects of the liberal and unsolicited support of their more prosperous neighbours'.[6]

Presenting periods of sickness as special circumstances which deviated from the norm helped to justify and validate the giving of charity through an organised society. Earlier forms of personal almsgiving had provided an element of supervision over the charitable gift allowing the benefactor to assess the situation of the recipient and to give - or not to give - as they saw fit. Similarly, members of the clergy and church elders oversaw the distribution of Kirk monies, the earliest form of organised charity. These individuals, who were entrusted with public monies through the authority of the Kirk, had immediate contact with the poor and again could judge the validity or worth of the claim. On the other hand, contributing money to an organised charitable society meant the placement of trust in a body of largely self-elected individuals, many of whom were ordinary members of the public whose ability to judge the worthiness of the claimants could be influenced by subjectivity and prejudice.

We might therefore ask, on what basis were contributors requested to endorse and sanction the activities of such charitable societies? Both the committee members of, and contributors to, such organisations tended to be drawn from the middle classes. This situation created something of an elite grouping. Personal and business contacts, extended into the realm of the organised charity, were essential to the creation of a feeling of trust. The involvement of official dignitaries or local worthies as patrons or committee members also added authority and credibility to the organisations. Furthermore, the fact that many of the early organised charities had a medical focus and concerned themselves with the sick eased the period of transition between the old and more personal, and the new and more organised forms of charitable giving. The sick and the diseased were the most worthy of charitable causes; it was easier to identify a sick person as a needy person and any anxieties over the level of trust which had to be placed by the contributors in the office-bearers of a charitable society were more easily reconciled.

'The want of an asylum for the insane was very much felt in Dundee'[7]

Both the Infirmary and the Asylum in Dundee had earlier origins than their dates of opening with the establishment of public subscriptions in 1792 and 1805 respectively. The Infirmary, eventually opened in 1798, was described as an institution which embraced 'at once several objects of charity' including the indigent sick who gained a 'warm, clean, comfortable habitation'; the diseased who gained 'the best' medical attention; and also the 'ignorant' who benefited from 'a useful religious and moral instruction'.[8] The Infirmary continued its development as a multi-functional establishment, providing for the town on several different levels including the organisation of a form of health insurance for the working classes and an active participation in public health measures. The 'Dundee Royal', alone of all the town's charities, received large-scale support from the working classes of Dundee and district.[9]

A new Infirmary building was opened at mid-century, largely made possible through the charitable bequest of James Soutar and his sister.[10] The foundation stone of the new building was laid in 1852 and the institution opened two years later.[11] The symbolic importance of the site of the new building, in its lofty and commanding position near to Dudhope Castle, demonstrates the central importance of these large institutional charities to the town. This kind of civic philanthropy helped to reinforce regional dominance, with the Infirmary attracting financial support not just from Dundee and its hinterland such as Longforgan and Lundie and Fowlis, but also from Blairgowrie and Alyth in Perthshire and across the Tay from Forgan in Fife. As the Dundee Royal established itself as the central focus of the area in terms of medical care the charity was simultaneously helping to ensure the continuation of Dundee's pre-eminence as one of the four major Scottish towns.

As early as 1796, when the Infirmary was not yet open to receive in-patients, a request had been made by one of the Infirmary governors that a lunatic 'be confined for a short time'.[12] However, it would be some years before a suitable building for the reception of the insane was established in Dundee. A subscription was begun in 1805 but the foundation stone was not laid until September 1812 and the institution itself did not open until 1820. A perhaps understandable degree of scepticism was voiced by the *Dundee Advertiser* in 1819 when it suggested that the 'splendid, and as yet useless building' appeared to be 'clear proof, if not of the sense, at least of the sauciness of our population', when with 'not one maniac within its walls' the Asylum was to borrow £1500 to furnish the building and cover the first year's expenses. The Asylum was eventually opened fifteen years after the initial subscription, on 1 April 1820, 'the anniversary of All Fools' - much to the amusement of the local press.[13]

The Lunatic Asylum was one of the most poorly supported charities in Dundee with subscriptions falling away only a very few years after its opening. However, the Asylum continued to operate through funds raised from the patients' board and the sale of goods made by the patients, although it continued to call itself a charity and to appeal to the public for voluntary contributions.[14] Meanwhile, the establishment of charities with a medical focus continued including the Eye Institution (1836) and the Medical and Surgical Dispensary and Vaccine Institution (1838). They were followed in the mid to late 1840s with the opening of the Institution for Diseases of the Chest (1844) and the Homeopathic Dispensary (1849).

'Friendless and outcast children...'[15]

Also included in this initial period of charitable activity was the founding of the Orphan Institution, the Infant Schools and the City Mission Association. Dundee was one of the earliest of the major Scottish cities to establish institutional care, independent of the Poor Law, for orphan children.[16] Described as 'an asylum for fatherless children, where withdrawn from the miseries and wants of a contaminating world, they are trained up for usefulness in after life', the Orphan Institution claimed that it would shape better servants, labourers and artisans while adamantly stressing that this would neither foster insubordination nor elevate anyone above his 'proper sphere'.[17] The Institution continued to prick the consciences of the Dundee townspeople through its literature. For example, the Annual Report of 1853 commented that some surprise might be expressed on discovering that in a manufacturing town of 80,000 inhabitants only twenty-three orphans were resident in the Orphan Institution:

> The number is indeed surprisingly small; but the Directors can
> assure you it is so not entirely because of the general prosperity
> of the town and prudent economy of the working classes, but
> because the more favoured portion of the community have for
> several years past made provision for only that number.[18]

Somewhat ironically, the model of virtuous morality, with its stress on proper positions and social obligations which the Institution held up to the orphans under their charge, appeared somewhat lacking in the example shown by the town's own middle class.

Despite the limitations of the Orphan Institution, children were a popular object for the ministrations of the nineteenth-century philanthropists and Dundee also boasted several infant schools. As with all the charities dealing with children the aim was to shape their present (and hopefully future) behaviour in line with middle-class mores. The infant schools were seen as a means of instructing children both in good habits and religion. A female-run philanthropic venture, the infant schools were part of a charitable out-reach into the 'poor man's country', something which the middle-class women in Dundee appeared more willing to take on than their male counterparts. The female committee members were also more flexible with their resources. For example, the Hawkhill school, while 'in the vicinity of a district mostly inhabited by the labouring classes', admitted the children of middle-class subscribers when places were available.[19]

A somewhat mixed bag of organisations and societies came to light in the late 1840s, including the Deaf and Dumb Institution, the Industrial Schools Society and the Model Lodging-House Association. The object of the Industrial Schools Society, established in 1846, was not dissimilar to that of the Orphan Institution in that its aims for the children included bringing them 'within the reach of religious instruction' and in 'train[ing] them up in habits of industry and usefulness'.[20] However, the section of the 'juvenile population' the Society aimed to reclaim from 'a course of vice and crime', and who were 'driven to our streets to seek the means of subsistence by beggary or crime', were more desperate than those sought out by the Orphan Institution, which continually emphasised respectability.[21] The Industrial Schools Society was the first charity in Dundee to address the real want and poverty which existed in the town, exemplified by the extremely impoverished and often criminal children of the streets. It would be wrong to assume that the poor condition of the children was the only, or even the main, motivating factor behind the establishment of the charity however, as the ultimate aim of the Society was to prevent these children from becoming inmates of the local gaol rather than simply to improve their socio-economic condition.

A moralising tone was never far distant, as when an annual report complained that the sub-committee had had to regulate the admission of children to the schools 'as many of the applicants were from a class quite different from that for whose benefit this Institution was established'.[22] It is difficult to ascertain from this comment exactly which class of children were applying for admission, but with the positive attraction of food freely available in the schools - 'the principal means' of attracting the children to the school and keeping them there - a wide range of children would probably have been sent to the institutions by their parents as a means of keeping them cheaply fed.[23] The refusal of the Society to be swayed or diverted from its stated object, regardless of any other apparent cases of need, provides a good example of the narrow view adopted by the charitable organisations.[24] However, limited funds meant only a restricted number could be given assistance and the proud statement that,

> [t]he effect [of the charity] on the town was very apparent...instead of the numbers of begging children who had

> previously infested the streets, in a short time scarcely one was to be seen,[25]

while a clear attempt at self-promotion and fund-raising, also demonstrates that it was the genuine underclass which the charity aimed to help.

A desire to reduce the high level of juvenile crime - a direct threat to the town's middle classes - was undoubtedly a strong motivating factor behind the establishment of the charity. The Society made great efforts to remove the children from what was seen as the morally contaminating influence of parents and associates. While the general public - the prospective supporters of the charity - were allowed regular admittance to the institution between 11am and 5pm three days a week, the parents and friends of the children were restricted to one visit every two months on strictly regulated dates and for restricted periods of time.[26]

In addition to practical means of attempting to reclaim the children by removing them from undesirable influences, symbolism was also employed. 'A suit of white moleskin' must have been highly unsuitable for 'the every-day attire of the boys', who were variously employed at making paper bags, coir mats and brushes and in preparing firewood for sale.[27] However, their white clothes represented their new and unblemished, almost holy, status - a blank sheet upon which the rest of their 'useful' lives could be written.[28]

National charities also had branches in Dundee, such as the Auxiliary Gaelic School Society (1817). Several other auxiliary societies were also established in the town, including the Dundee Auxiliary Colonial Society (c.1834) and the Shipwrecked Fishermen and Mariners' Benevolent Society (c.1847). The variety of later charitable developments in the town after mid-century included the Cottage Home in Strawberry Bank (1875) which provided a Christian environment for pauper and neglected children; the Cabman's Shelter (1875) set on iron wheels and designed to be mobile; the British Workman (1875) a seventy-year old public house transformed into a temperance club; and the Flower Mission to the Sick Poor which collected several thousand bouquets every summer for distribution to the homes of the poor.

Limited support was provided to some of these new charities as with the Flower Mission which succeeded in raising only three pounds in subscriptions in 1890.[29] However, some of the new charities were innovatory, for example, the Day Nursery (1874) established by a few gentlemen to provide care, between 5.30 am and 6.30 pm, for young children whose mothers were employed in the public works.[30] Others were viewed as contentious. It was considered by some that the Prisoner's Aid Society (1872), which offered help in finding work but also provided ready money, might only serve to attract ex-convicts into the town. The information from the 1875 Perth Prison Report that fifteen of the sixty released prisoners had set off for Dundee was felt to be 'ominous'.[31]

The nature of the charities which were established in Dundee in the first half of the nineteenth century appear to bear little direct relevance to local conditions in the town, such as the needs of a large female working population. Meanwhile some organisations, such as the Auxiliary Gaelic Schools Society, supported charitable activity which was largely based outwith the town. The growing number of medical charities founded in the 1830s and 1840s, particularly the Eye Institution and the Institution for Diseases of the Chest, were the only examples of organised charity which could be said to have been responding directly to the needs of the urban-industrial community in that period. It was only as mid-century approached that a charitable response to the social conditions in Dundee appeared to take place, with the establishment of organisations such as the Model Lodging-House Association and the Industrial Schools.

Many of the charities founded in this period were overtly controlling, however, rather than simply part of a spontaneous 'humanitarian' response to a perceived need. The Industrial Schools and the Lodging-House Association - which provided a middle-class 'model' type of housing for the working classes - could both be included in this category. In reality much of nineteenth-century charitable development in Dundee, rather than representing any direct response to the immediate wants or needs of the town's lower classes, represented an answer to the concerns of the middle-class community for whom the way of life of the street children, the wandering insane, the moral and spiritual welfare of the working classes, and the condition of the poor generally caused anxiety or revulsion.

Notes

1 W. Norrie, *Norrie's Handbook to Dundee Past and Present* (1876), 125.

2 Examples of charities founded prior to 1820 in Glasgow include the University Lying-In Hospital (1792), Infirmary (1792), Female Society (1799), Sick and Destitute Strangers' Friend Society (1803), Lock Hospital (1805), Benevolent Society for Clothing the Poor (1812), Lunatic Asylum (1814) and Magdalene Asylum (1815). In Edinburgh they include the Infirmary (1729), Public Dispensary (1776), Society for Relief of the Destitute Sick (1785), Blind Asylum (1792), Magdalene Asylum (1797), House of Industry (1801) and Lunatic Asylum (1813). Aberdeen's include the Infirmary (*c.* 1739), Dispensary (1781), Sick Man's Friend Society (1792), Lunatic Asylum (1800), Female Society (1805), Deaf and Dumb Institution (1817), Clothing Society (1817), Asylum for the Blind (1818). See L. Walsh, 'The Development of Organised Charity in the Scottish Burgh. Dundee 1790-1850' (unpublished PhD thesis, University of Dundee, 1997), Appendix I, for full details of Dundee charities founded in this period.

3 StAUA, M415, DRI, Minute Book, Vol. 1, General Meeting, 10 June 1799.

4 LS, Pamphlets D4488, Regulations of the Society for Relief of the Indigent Sick (1819).

5 *Ibid.*

6 *Ibid.*

7 DARC, *Handbook.*

8 Dundee University Archives [DUA], THB 1/2/2, DRI, *Annual Report* (1832).

9 See Walsh, 'The Development of Organised Charity'.

10 DARC, *Handbook.*

11 *Ibid.*

12 StAUA, M 415, DRI, Minute Book, 31 October, 1796.

13 LS, L.Coll. 279(2), extract from the *Dundee Advertiser*, 1820.

14 See Walsh, 'The Development of Organised Charity', 130-168.

15 DARC, *Handbook.*

16 Although it has previously been recorded that the Orphan Institution was founded as the result of the sinking of a pinnace in the Tay (see for example, 'Tay Disaster that gave Dundee an Orphanage', *Evening Telegraph*, 10 September 1965), this was not the case as discussions were underway regarding the founding of the Institution prior to the maritime accident. I am grateful to Jerry Wright for first drawing my attention to this point.

17 DARC, GD/DOI/5/1, DROI, Directors' Reports, 1830-1919, 1839; LS, Pamphlets D4485, DROI, *Annual Report* (1816).

18 DARC, GD/DO1/5/1, DROI, Directors Reports, 1830-1919, 1853.

19 LS, L.Coll. 213(9A), *Report of the Committee of the Dundee Infant Schools* (1829, 1831).

[20] LS, L.Coll. 41(2), Dundee Industrial Schools Society [DISS], *Annual Report* (1847).

[21] See Walsh, 'The Development of Organised Charity', 203-208.

[22] LS, L.Coll. 41(2), DISS, *Annual Report* (1847).

[23] See Walsh, 'The Development of Organised Charity', 203-208.

[24] Prospective applicants to a particular charity were often prevented from obtaining relief if they were in receipt of assistance from another charity. In 1837 five pensioners were struck off the roll of the Dundee Female Society [DFS], having received aid from Petrie's Mortification. LS, L.Coll. 55(13), DFS, *Annual Report* (1837).

[25] LS, L.Coll. 41(2), DISS, *Annual Report* (1847).

[26] LS, L.Coll. 41(3), DISS, *Annual Report* (1876).

[27] LS, L.Coll. 41(7), cuttings relating to the Industrial Schools; LS, L.Coll. 41(3), DISS, *Annual Report* (1876).

[28] The white clothing could also have been part of a stigmatisation of the children. Until 1856 Dundee's parish poor were buried in white coffins. LS, L.Coll. Box 398, 'Biographical Details'.

[29] *Dundee Year Book 1890.*

[30] DARC, *Handbook*

[31] *Ibid.*

Chapter 3

A Middle-Class Venture

'In Dundee...while it also has its charities which owe their origin to individual philanthropy -
such institutions as the Royal Infirmary, the Industrial Schools, or the Orphan Institution, are
not the result of isolated benevolence, but the work of an equally diffused goodness of heart.'[1]

Much of the support for the Dundee charities, in the form of organisation and funding, originated with a relatively small group of mainly middle-class individuals who also held other positions of authority or influence in the town's economic, civic or religious life. Their activity was remarkable not only in terms of the funds which were raised, but also in the personal time which was given and the responsibility which was undertaken on behalf of the new charitable organisations. These individuals undertook this charitable work in a field of activity where the only previous form of organised philanthropy in the town had consisted of little more than the administration of the Hospital and Kirk monies. The only other sources of funds were a limited number of mortifications (or endowed funds) controlled by the Kirk, Town Council and to a lesser extent the Trades, whose charity was largely distributed to the poor and the needy in their own homes through the traditional routes of clergy or town officials.

Organised charity provided a vehicle for the distribution of charitable monies which appealed to prospective subscribers on several levels. Recognition of individual charitable acts was guaranteed through the publication of subscription lists, even on the basis of relatively small amounts, while larger sums could warrant a mention in the local press or inclusion on an inscribed board of contributors' names. The subscriber also had the opportunity to control the destination of his charitable contribution, whether for general poor relief or perhaps for orphans or medical care. Neither of these opportunities was provided through the general voluntary contributions collected and dispersed by the Kirk. Power and control were also given to the subscriber in that by giving or withholding his contribution he had the ability, or the perceived ability, to influence the lives and well being of others. These opportunities provided the basis of an appeal which aimed to encourage an increased level of philanthropy based on something other than simple humanitarianism.

Charitable development in this period was focused on urban areas and urban dwellers. (Apart from the obvious exceptions of the anti-slavery societies and overseas missions. There appears to have been very few charities that dealt with rural affairs in this period, although the Auxiliary Gaelic Schools could perhaps be included in this category.) The focus of philanthropic activity on the towns and cities of the late eighteenth and nineteenth centuries indicates that the ideologies generated or discussed within these urban areas had a significant role to play in the charitable impulse. The central importance of the urban middle class to such ventures also indicates that such ideologies had to have a strong appeal to this group. One such ideology was evangelicalism.

The persuasion of piety

The relatively early establishment of the Dundee City Mission in 1830 (the city missions of Glasgow and Edinburgh, both considerably larger urban areas than Dundee, were opened in 1826 and 1832 respectively) and the existence of previous mission societies in the town from the early years of the nineteenth century, reinforces the strong religious element which appears to have pervaded at least part of the nineteenth-century Dundee community - but not all. The society's first report described the origins of the charity:

> A few individuals convinced that many of the inhabitants of this Town seldom, if ever, attend any Place of Worship; that a great deal of ignorance concerning the Gospel prevails among them, and that Christians generally, while making exertions for the spiritual interests of the Heathen abroad, have not paid sufficient attention to the equally pressing necessities of multitudes of our growing population at home, felt it their duty to endeavour to get a *City Mission* established in Dundee.[2]

While the establishment of the City Mission may have been triggered by general evangelical enthusiasm it was also the case, however, that such an impulse could result in a certain reluctance to give to organised charity. Thomas Chalmers, perhaps the most well known Scottish evangelical of the period, was most concerned that the Christian should be:

> discriminating in his donations to charity, preferring to give to individual cases where he was sure of the need, as opposed to large public bodies which could more easily be taken in by malingerers since they had so many applications to cope with.[3]

Chalmers also felt that 'public societies for the relief of the poor...should do their utmost to scrutinise their applicants, but [that] ultimately these societies should be abolished'.[4]

Clergymen in Dundee were, however, amongst those most actively involved in the solicitation of contributions for charitable organisations. The Rev. Heneage Horsley was amongst the four gentlemen whose exertions in soliciting subscriptions for the Dundee Infirmary in 1829 were particularly commended.[5] Suggestions were even made for suitable sums for donation. The system of 'guinea governorship' operated by many of the town's charities such as the Infirmary, which allowed the subscriber to recommend a certain number of individuals in direct relation to the amount of money subscribed, explicitly encouraged certain levels of contribution. Medical charities often do appear to have proved the exception to the rule and it was the Dundee Infirmary, out of all the town's charities, which benefited most from charitable contributions rooted in piety. Even such a strict adherent to evangelical doctrine as Thomas Chalmers made contributions to medical charities despite his misgivings over organised philanthropy, viewing such activity as a reflection of Christ's own actions in relieving the sick.[6]

However, Evangelicalism, and religion in general, was only one of many factors which influenced charitable giving in the nineteenth century. Others included Enlightenment philosophy, Utilitarianism and the 'science' of philanthropy itself. The ideas they advanced were eagerly seized upon by the urban middle classes and debated in a wide range of societies. The freedom of thought generated in this atmosphere led some, such as Charles W. Boase, to experiment and embrace new religions. Boase, a banker in Dundee and prominent supporter of several of the town's charities, was involved in the establishment of the new Christian or Catholic Apostolic Church (c.1836).[7] Much of the attractiveness of these philosophies, religious or otherwise, appears to have rested as much in the purveyors of the message as in the message itself. The Rev. R.M. McCheyne, perhaps Dundee's most influential evangelical clergyman, had a congregation of approximately 1100 in the late 1830s, one third of which came from outwith his immediate parish of St Peters.[8] As was the case with Thomas Chalmers, followers were prepared to travel extensively to hear popular evangelical preachers such as Cheyne, implying that their ministry had become as much fashion as religion, and part of the 'pick and mix' of early nineteenth-century ideology.

Although a mixture of influences and ideologies were important in the generation of the charitable impulse, charities were unlikely to readily associate themselves with a particular group or religious denomination as this association could inhibit voluntary charity. During the selection process for a teacher for the Orphan Institution one of the candidates, an Antiburgher, stepped down due to the stipulation that he attend the Established Church with the children.[9] There was also a split in the Infant Schools Society over the dominance of members of the Established Church. The promoters of the New Infant Schools Society, formed as a result of the division, regretted that such a situation should have arisen 'more especially as it seems quite unconnected with the instruction of Infant children, - a work in which Christians may certainly combine without any compromise of principle.' One of the resolutions of the new society was that 'nothing denominational or sectarian' was to be introduced into the children's religious instruction.[10] Many of the organisations went out of their way to demonstrate that their charity was completely non-sectarian, such as the Clothing Society which described itself as a 'perfectly unsectarian' organisation.[11] A further example is provided by the City Mission Association which, although decidedly evangelical in nature, proclaimed itself dedicated to 'reading and explaining the word of God without the least tinge of sectarianism', their missionaries visiting families of 'all denominations'.[12]

The town's charities appear to have accepted persons of all denominations as recipients of their funds, although this was sometimes not without criticism. It was reported in 1848 that a 'vulgar prejudice' had begun against the Infirmary on account of allegations that it had been converted into a 'receptacle only of Irish paupers'.[13] The Institution for the Reformation of Females (commonly shortened to 'The Home') also found itself in some difficulty over the issue of Catholic inmates, noting in its first annual report that 'almost the only difficulty [was] the diversity of opinion upon religious subjects'. While 'determined that all should be received' nevertheless 'some restrictions' were to be made 'in the case of the Roman Catholic inmates'.[14] The large number of Catholic Irish immigrants in Dundee would have formed a considerable percentage of the town's needy cases. It was not until the second half of the nineteenth century that a branch of the St Vincent de Paul Society (a Roman Catholic organisation which cared for the poor and needy) was established in Dundee.

Prominent members of the Catholic clergy, such as Bishop Paterson who gave a charity sermon in Dundee in 1831, were occasionally invited to preach on behalf of the town's charitable organisations.[15] One historian, commenting on the involvement of members of the Catholic Church's hierarchy in Edinburgh's charitable bodies, has argued that rather than an expression of religious tolerance the acceptance, or even encouragement, of Catholic involvement came as a consequence of economics. The charities sought the financial support of the Catholic congregations and in return promised relief to Catholics in need.[16] It is difficult to apply this argument to Dundee, however, as there was only one Catholic chapel in the town until as late as

1835, when St Andrew's Cathedral was built. Also, it is likely that the majority of Catholic immigrants in Dundee would have been financially unable - or perhaps unwilling - to become regular contributors to the town's charities. The one exception to this again appears to have been the Infirmary which received contributions raised by church collections from the Catholic chapel from at least as early as 1825.[17] The Infirmary was proving to be distinct and unique among the organised charities of the town in its ability to stimulate the charitable impulse of the townspeople of Dundee, and to attract both a diverse and sustained level of support from many denominations.

'[No Agents] to introduce...the peculiarities of any sect or party whatever to those whom he may have occasion to visit'[18]

Despite the importance of the role played by charitable foundations in the welfare and shaping of urban communities, the establishment of these organisations could be quite arbitrary and was often reliant on current fashionable trends in philanthropy and the precedent of similar activity in other towns. This somewhat precarious situation concerning the social and civic development of towns such as Dundee was further compounded by incidents such as the Disruption of 1843. At the Disruption, six of the seventeen Church of Scotland congregations in Dundee 'came out' and became part of the new Free Church.[19] This meant that the middle classes - those individuals who comprised the main church-going body in the town - had themselves also been divided. Elements of the middle class had been divided previously, particularly over issues relating to local politics, but the importance of the Disruption lay in its ability to affect both men and women, the old and the young, the politically minded and the non-politically minded. This division affected essentially what was the largest source of charitable funds in the city - the church-going middle class.

The effect of the Disruption on middle-class levels of support and involvement in Dundee's organised charities was not immediately apparent. Difficulties had occasionally arisen over denominational aspects of charitable activity but, as has been seen, the majority of the Dundee charities regularly went out of their way to declare the non-sectarian nature of their activities. This may have helped to reduce any potential friction between members of the Kirk and the Free Church in their continuing support of the town's charities. The practical consequences of the Disruption meant that new areas in need of middle-class support were created as a result of the demand for new church buildings. Nineteen new churches were built in Dundee between 1850 and 1900 as a result of the division within the Church of

Scotland.[20] This building programme undoubtedly diverted a considerable amount of disposable income away from the town's charities.[21] Furthermore, a row over the Dundee Town Council's reluctance to release monies formerly used for Church of Scotland clergy stipends lasted for some thirty years following the Disruption. The result was that a great deal of attention and energy was diverted from other needy causes in the town.[22]

One such casualty of the Disruption may have been the Seamen's Friend Society. Although Dundee was a thriving port the number of established charities which were associated with the welfare of seafarers was relatively small. The Dundee Seamen's Friend Society was founded in 1838, with the aim to promote 'the religious & moral instruction of the Sailors of this Port'. Some years prior to this a society had opened a place of worship near the harbour for use by seamen but lack of financial support had resulted in its demise. The Seamen's Friend Society was not to prove any more successful than the earlier venture and was dissolved in 1843. The reasons for this are not clear, but they were not the result of an immediate lack of funds. The Society enjoyed the patronage of the provost and magistrates of the town while Thomas Erskine of Linlathen, a well-known supporter of Dundee charities in both organisational and financial terms, held the position of president. The Society boasted a ladies committee and a missionary in addition to a fund of almost £1,000 by 1841, raised with the view to building a Mariners' Church.

By 1843, however, the Society had been dissolved, the subscriptions repaid and the plans to build a church abandoned, indicating that the Society may have been a casualty of the Disruption of that same year. The Society was primarily a religious charity. The recipients of the calling notice for the organisation's original meeting had included thirteen clergymen, several of whom would probably have become involved with the Society. They may have held differing views on the Disruption and the direction the Seamen's Friend Society should subsequently take. (It is possible that the plan for the church was later resurrected by some of the subscribers, as a Mariner's Free Church was built in the town).

Conversely, the heady atmosphere of religious rivalry may also have encouraged individuals to ever-greater displays of charitable benevolence. In 1856 David Baxter (of the famous Dundee textile manufacturing firm) purchased the estate of Kilmaron near Cupar in Fife and subsequently he attended and became a generous benefactor of the Free Church in Cupar.[23] While Baxter had been a regular contributor to many of Dundee's charities prior to the Disruption period, his most munificent gestures follow that date. In 1860 he was the main motivating force behind the establishment of the Convalescent House, contributing £10,000 to the charitable fund himself and helping to raise subscriptions from his friends towards the completion of the project.[24] A year later Baxter announced that he, with his sister Mary Ann, was to gift land to the value of £50,000 to the people of Dundee as a public park.[25] Although the motivating factors behind charitable gestures were diverse, it is highly likely that such an important change in the religious life of an individual - particularly as religion and benevolence were so intimately associated - could stimulate charitable giving.

Philanthropy as fashion

Many contemporaries viewed Church going as a social event and public gatherings of all kinds were a fashionable method of motivating prospective charitable contributors. Balls, in aid of the poor generally or for specific charities, were held occasionally in early nineteenth-century Dundee. For example, a ball organised in aid of the Orphan Institution appears to have become an annual event by the 1820s.[26] It was still taking place in 1839 although the funds raised in that year amounted to just over the relatively small sum of fourteen pounds.[27] The Dundee Female Society stopped holding its annual ball in the late 1820s, perhaps due to a disappointing financial return, and began to publish annual reports instead.[28] Published literature of this kind was viewed as a potentially more successful fund-raising strategy.

Indeed, the amount of money raised from events such as balls compared badly with that realised from more lowbrow forms of entertainment. While the ball held at the Thistle Hall in 1838, to raise funds 'to supply the pressing wants of the unemployed poor' realised thirty pounds, a benefit hosted by Cooke's Circus two years previously had raised over forty-six pounds.[29] Events such as circuses, exhibitions and public lectures proved the more popular fund-raising events in the town. Mr Springthorpe's exhibition of composition figures, Mr Ord's Olympic Circus, and Mr Addison's show of prize oxen all raised money for the Infirmary in 1829-30.[30] Although strictly regarded as incidental funds, these contributions could become quite regular, as was demonstrated by Mr Springthorpe's wax figures which were again exhibited for the benefit of the Infirmary in 1833-34, and which allowed a wider spectrum of people to become involved as contributors.

Social and business connections between individuals were important in building up a charity subscription list. This began at the very basic level of providing a safe and respectable place, often a shop, for the receipt of contributions and the opportunity to recommend individuals to a particular charity. George Scott's High Street shop acted as a repository for the 'Gifts of the Benevolent, in articles of bedding & c.', to the Orphan Institution.[31] The Dundee Female Society advised prospective contributors that a 'particular account' of the charity could be seen at the shops of William Webster, William Pitcairn and Thomas Hunter in the High Street where subscriptions and donations would also be received. Meanwhile, interested parties were given the opportunity to view the accounts of the Society for Relief of the Indigent Sick at the Exchange Coffee Rooms, where subscribers were also able to recommend individuals to the charity.[32] Connections made through church membership could also prove useful. Church premises could be used for annual meetings, whilst also conveniently providing a suitable place to hear the annual sermon. The Orphan Institution held its 1817 annual meeting in the West Port Chapel, where the anniversary sermon was read.[33] A continuing link of the charity with this congregation is also reflected in the several collections made at the Chapel in the 1830s for the same body.[34]

The involvement of the middle classes, and particularly the merchant class, in the charitable and civic institutions of Dundee facilitated the development of their identity as an important social, as well as economic, group within the town. The emergence of a middle-class charitable elite - of both men and women - ensured, however, that such involvement was concentrated in a distinct section of the community. Contact with the upper and working classes, and the ability of the middle-class charitable elite to construct relationships with these groups, was largely facilitated through their involvement in the town's organised charities in terms of their authority, influence and civic standing.

Notes

[1] DARC, *Handbook*

[2] LS, L.Coll. 105(6), Dundee City Mission Association [DCMA], *Annual Report* (*c.* 1830).

[3] M.T. Furgol, 'Thomas Chalmers' poor relief theories and their implementation in the early nineteenth century' (unpublished PhD thesis, University of Edinburgh, 1987), 38.

[4] Furgol, 'Thomas Chalmers', 38-39.

[5] LS, L.Coll. 404(1), DRI, *Annual Report* (1829).

[6] B. Hilton, *The Age of Atonement. The Influence of Evangelicalism on Social and Economic Thought, 1795-1865* (Oxford, 1988), 85.

[7] LS, L.Coll. 100(1), cuttings concerning the Catholic Apostolic Church including the obituary of C.W. Boase.

[8] W. Norrie, *Dundee Celebrities* (Dundee, 1873), 82.

[9] DARC, GD/AY/7/1/1, DROI, Minute Book, 1815-1823, 31 August 1815.

[10] LS, L.Coll. *Report of the New Infant School Society* (c. 1839-40).

[11] Norrie, *Norrie's Handbook*

[12] LS, L.Coll. 279(16), ms concerning the City Mission Association; LS, L.Coll. 272(2), Journal of City Missionary.

[13] DUA, THB 1/2/2, DRI, *Annual Report* (1848).

[14] Dundee University Library, Br 252.03 M 752, *Report of The Home, an Institution for the Reformation of Females* (1849).

[15] I am grateful to Richard MacCready for drawing this point to my attention. The sermon may have aided the fortunes of the charity but it did little for the health of the Bishop, who collapsed and died a few hours later. P.F. Anson, *The Catholic Church in Modern Scotland 1580-1937* (London, 1937), 114.

[16] C. Johnson, *Developments in the Roman Catholic Church in Scotland 1789-1829* (Edinburgh, 1983), 173.

[17] LS, L.Coll. 404(2), DRI, *Annual Report* (1825).

[18] LS, L.Coll. 105(6), DCMA, *Annual Report* (c.1830).

[19] Whatley et. al., *Life and Times*, 110.

[20] *Ibid.*

[21] For a demonstration of the sums of money that were raised by the Free Church throughout Scotland for church building, and for other purposes including education and missions, see T. Brown, *Annals of the Disruption* (Edinburgh, 1893), Appendix III.

[22] E. Gauldie, *The Dundee Textile Industry 1790-1885 (from the papers of Peter Carmichael of Arthurstone)*, 98 (footnote).

[23] Norrie, *Dundee Celebrities*, 405-6.

[24] Norrie, *Dundee Celebrities*, 405; DARC, *Handbook*

[25] DUA, MS 105, Minute Book of the Baxter Park, No. 1.

[26] DARC, GD/AY/7/1/1, DROI, Minute Book, 1815-23, 13 April 1822.

[27] DARC, GD/DO1/5/1, DROI, *Directors' Reports, 1830-1919* (1839).

[28] LS, Pamphlets D4487I, DFS, *Annual Report* (1828).

[29] LS, A.C. Lamb and A.H. Millar (eds.), *Annals of Dundee being Extracts from the "Dundee Advertiser" 1801-1840* (1908), 320-21.

[30] LS, L.Coll. 404(1), DRI, *Annual Report* (1830).

[31] DARC, GD/AY/7/1/1, DROI, Minute Book, 1815-1823, 21 June 1815.

[32] *Dundee Advertiser*, 14 December 1804; 8 February 1805.

[33] *Dundee Advertiser*, 6 October 1817.

[34] DARC, CH/14/4/32, Account Book of the West Port Chapel, 1826-1833.

Chapter 4

Patrons and Profit

'[The Secretary to write to the Right Honourable the Earl of Airlie and] respectfully to solicit
his Lordship to contribute to the funds such a sum as he may incline' [1]

Although the middle classes dominated the day-to-day organisation and
management of the town's charities, the upper classes continued to have a role to
play for a large part of the nineteenth century. Members of the gentry made occasional,
often quite magnificent gestures, to the local charities such as the 100 guineas donated
to the Lunatic Asylum by the Earl of Strathmore in 1815.[2] The level of their
involvement, however, did not always match that which was expected of them.
Rev. Small, commenting upon the recent establishment of the town's Dispensary,
noted that:

> The president and principal benefactor is Lord Douglas. But
> the contributions of the remaining heritors, (a very few
> excepted,) either to this or to any other charitable institutions
> of the place, notwithstanding all the advantages they derive
> from it, are hardly worth the mentioning.[3]

Certainly, such grand gestures from the gentry were most likely to be forthcoming
when the individual also occupied a figurehead position within a charity. The Earl
of Strathmore was vice-president of the Infirmary when he made his donation of
100 guineas.[4] Similarly, the donation of five guineas to the Orphan Institution from
Lady Duncan in September 1819 preceded her appointment as patroness of the
charity in November of that year.[5] Upper-class subscribers tended to congregate
together in charities such as 'The Caledonian Asylum, for Educating and Supporting
such Children of Soldiers, Sailors, and Marines, natives of Scotland, as cannot be
admitted into the royal institutions of Chelsea and Greenwich; and of indigent Scots
parents, resident in London, not entitled to parochial relief'. A notice of subscribers
to this charity was inserted in the *Dundee Advertiser* on several occasions, revealing
an extensive list which appeared to contain most of the British aristocracy and other
notables such as Members of Parliament, in addition to large sections of the Royal
family, including the Prince Regent as patron.[6]

On a local scale such opportunities presented themselves in the form of Dundee's institutional charities, such as the Infirmary, the Lunatic Asylum and the Orphan Institution. Patronage from the gentry was also given to some of the smaller of the town's charities, although these were often auxiliary branches of national organisations with a relatively high profile. The upper classes generally played a less significant role in the smaller charities, although one exception to this was the Ogilvy family. The Institution for the Reformation of Females had been founded under the patronage of several female members of the gentry, including Lady Jane Ogilvy and Lady Kinnaird, in addition to its royal patroness, the Duchess of Kent. The Home was also significant in that it demonstrated a more active upper-class involvement in the affairs and management of the day-to-day running of the organisation, with Lady Jane Ogilvy herself included amongst the members of the committee of management for its first year.[7]

There were several upper-class contributors to The Home, including the Earl of Airlie, Lady Scott of Ancrum and Balgay, and Sir James Ramsay of Banff. Lady Jane Ogilvy was particularly generous in her annual subscription of forty pounds, although several other upper-class contributions raised from friends or acquaintances outside the town appear relatively unremarkable, such as the four pounds donation and one pound annual subscription from the Ladies Fanny and Mary Howard of London or the five pounds donations from the Earls of Suffolk and Roden. The Ogilvys were occasional philanthropists in early nineteenth-century Dundee - making such contributions as five pounds to the Orphan Institution in 1818 - although Lady Ogilvy became particularly active at mid-century, going on to found an orphanage for imbecile children on her lands at Baldovan in 1855, to which Queen Victoria contributed £100.[8]

A more regular, and perhaps exceptional, contributor from the 'better classes' of Dundee and district was William Ramsay Maule, later Lord Panmure, whose generosity towards charitable organisations extended throughout Forfarshire. This generosity contrasted sharply with his somewhat volatile nature. Described as a 'very powerful and conspicuous personality' whose temper could be 'overbearing, and, when crossed, ungovernable', William Ramsay Maule was also one of the most generous philanthropists Dundee and its surrounding area has ever known.[9] Born in 1771, Maule was one of the last of an era of landed gentry whose omnipresence was rapidly becoming overshadowed by socio-economic and political changes and from a rural to an urban world, all of which were accompanied by the rise of the bourgeoisie. Maule's career included a spell in the army and time spent on the political battlefield as Member of Parliament for Forfarshire, before being raised to the peerage in 1831. A man of violent temper and immovable opinion with regard to his family, Maule was feted in public for his generous acts of charity.

During the early nineteenth century William Maule made regular contributions to numerous charitable organisations in Dundee including the Infirmary, the Lunatic Asylum, the Orphan Institution and the Female Society, in addition to the charities of towns in the region such as Arbroath and Brechin. His generosity outlived his parliamentary career - and his life in the form of legacies - and continued as a form of civic paternalism through which he organised long-term support for many of Dundee's charities. In 1838, for example, he made a donation of £1,000 to the Town Council to be known as the Panmure Endowment, 'upon a bond being granted to the directors of the Infirmary, binding the town in all time coming to pay £50 per annum to that Institution'.[10]

The Dundee charities were more than eager to recognise publicly Lord Panmure's generosity. Following the establishment of the Panmure Endowment the committee members of the Infirmary proposed raising a subscription towards the commissioning of a portrait or some other 'permanent memorial' in his honour. The 'Noble Lord' had anticipated such an event, however, and donated a portrait of himself to the Institution. Regardless of this event the subscription continued with a view to commissioning a bust of Panmure in order to 'associate his name with this place as one of the most liberal patrons of its public charities'.[11] Many of the surrounding towns, such as Carnoustie and Brechin, added to this immortalisation by naming streets after the generous benefactor, with Panmure Street in Dundee opened in 1839 in recognition of his 'recent munificent donations to the funds of the infirmary'.[12]

Having a titled patron was an undeniable asset to charities of the period. Panmure was the life patron of the Medical and Surgical Dispensary and Vaccine Institution in Dundee; the president of the Dundee auxiliary branch of the Shipwrecked Fishermen and Mariners' Benevolent Society; the president of the Orphan Institution for the periods 1830-41 and 1841-52 in conjunction with the Earl of Airlie; and was unanimously elected president of the Brechin Dispensary at its inception in 1823, a position he was to hold until at least 1847.[13] Panmure, however, was more than just a figurehead to these charitable organisations. Included amongst the gifts he bestowed upon the Brechin Mechanics' Institute were several paintings, a hall in which to hang them and a separate donation of £1000.[14] The Home, of which Panmure was patron alongside his contemporaries the Earl of Airlie and Sir John Ogilivy, was in receipt of his generosity to an extent unrivalled by his co-patrons. At the opening, Panmure gave a donation of £100 to the institution in addition to an annual subscription of fifty pounds. This generosity can be compared with the Earl of Airlie's twenty pounds donation and ten pounds subscription. Panmure's contribution was far and away the largest of that year.[15]

A plan into which the appropriate influential individuals could be fitted was often sketched out by the larger charitable organisations. The annual report of the Dundee Lunatic Asylum stipulated the following: extraordinary directors were to include the Lord Lieutenant of the County of Forfar, Member of Parliament for Forfar, Sheriff-Depute of the County of Forfar, Member of Parliament for Dundee (the Asylum was obviously planning ahead as Dundee did not achieve separate political representation until 1832), Moderator of the Synod of Angus and the Mearns, plus four named directors for life. Ordinary directors were to include for the Town Council (*ex-officio*), the Provost, 'oldest Bailie', Dean of Guild, three members from the Nine Trades, one member from the Three Trades, four members of the Guildry, one member of the Seamen Fraternity, a representative for the lodges and societies in Dundee, two members of the Kirk Session, two members from the Presbytery, four individuals representing the County of Forfar and eight individuals chosen from the governors of the Dundee Royal Infirmary.[16] This list of office-bearers appears to have covered all of the areas of influence, and not incidentally sources of funds, within the Dundee community and indicates that although a titled figurehead was desirable, increasingly there were many other urban sources of influence and power and financial support.

The new urban-industrial philanthropists, and often their whole families, were of central importance to many of Dundee's charities. One such family in Dundee were the Baxters, whose textile-manufacturing firm was one of the most important and influential in the town. The family was headed by William Baxter of Ellengowan (and later of Balgavies). His four sons Edward, David (later Sir David Baxter of Kilmaron), John Gorrill and William Gorrill all had interests in the family business. William Baxter & Son became Baxter Brothers in 1825 when the two younger sons were taken into the family business.[17] William Baxter's daughters and his brother, John Baxter of Idvies, were also important figures in the charitable organisations of the town. As men of power and influence within the community the Baxters' involvement in the town's charities was both expected and anticipated. Without the financial, organisational and motivational support which these men and women provided, several of the town's charities would have faced insurmountable difficulties.

The Baxter family as a whole, but particularly Edward Baxter, were closely involved with the City Mission Association. By 1834 Edward had assumed the position of president of the Association, and it was one which he continued to hold almost continuously at least until mid-century. Baxter's contribution to the charity was more important than simply that of being an office-bearer or figurehead. His annual subscription of ten guineas was easily the most important regular contribution to the Mission, while his substantial supplementary donation of thirty pounds per annum (from at least as early as 1840) would also have made a very welcome contribution to the Association's funds.[18]

In common with the older landed philanthropists of the late eighteenth and early nineteenth centuries, Edward Baxter's generosity may have been the direct result of his position as president of the charity. Usually, this was also the response of other individuals. For example, Andrew Low, who had long filled the role of vice-president, took over as president of the City Mission for a year in 1847 (Edward Baxter took over the role of one of the vice-presidents in that year, perhaps due to temporary pressing commitments in other areas of his life, as he was returned again as president in 1848). Low's subscription for 1847 was ten pounds, a contribution whose size was usually only equalled by either Edward Baxter or his father, whereas in 1837, when Low had held the position of vice-president, his subscription had been only six guineas.[19] Edward Baxter, however, appears to have taken a consistently generous interest in the City Mission. In 1847, although he had stepped down as president, his subscription remained at ten guineas and his annual donation remained at thirty pounds. He also made a further contribution of eleven pounds to a newly established fund to support the work of a seventh missionary in the town. Only three others gave additional support to this fund - Lord Kinnaird who subscribed ten pounds and P.H. Thoms (another vice-president) who subscribed five pounds. The remaining contribution of thirteen pounds came from Baxter Brothers & Co.[20]

Indeed, the Baxter family as a whole were a significant force in the funding of the City Mission. In 1837 the collective subscriptions to the charity from eight members of the immediate family came to more than twenty-five pounds.[21] Ten years later the sum subscribed by the family was over forty-five pounds.[22] In addition to Edward Baxter's regular and supplementary donations, the Baxter family contributions in 1847 amounted to little short of one hundred pounds. This was more than one third of the total amount of funds raised for the charity in that year, of £292 9s 6d.[23] The family's influence also affected the flow of other smaller donations which came to the charity, with the Baxter's Dens Mills Sabbath Schools making small but regular donations throughout the 1840s.[24]

Individuals could also have a major impact on charities by withholding their support. Lord Panmure appears never to have made a contribution to the City Mission

Association in any shape or form, which makes it one of the few charities to which he did not lend his support. As a charity with strong religious foundations, the City Mission received surprisingly few contributions from clergymen, a consistently useful source of funds for the city's charities, and relatively few legacies. The legacies which the City Mission did receive were also small in amount. Two pounds were bequeathed in 1842 and ten shillings in 1844. The most substantial legacy in this period came from a Baxter; Miss Margaret Baxter of Ellengowan left fifty pounds to the City Mission in 1845.[25]

The influence wielded by these important individuals or families could also adversely affect the fortunes of the town's charities beyond the impact of withholding their own personal subscriptions. In the first two years following the opening of the Lunatic Asylum in 1820, the charity boasted a relatively healthy list of contributors. In the institution's annual report of 1822 the list of supporters was noted as having raised more than £500 over the previous year. By 1823-24, however, that previously healthy list of contributors had been decimated. Although £356 was raised through contributions in that year, the figures were misleading. Almost £300 of the total had been secured through legacies, leaving just over thirty-six pounds in donations and just less than twenty pounds in subscriptions.[26] Something had occurred in the interim period to cause support for the Lunatic Asylum to collapse.[27] One possible reason was personal antagonism.

Edward Baxter was actively involved in the agitation to repeal the Linen Stamping Act and, as a result of this involvement, he came into conflict with David Blair, the Stamp-master in Dundee and Surveyor-General for Stamp-masters in Scotland. Blair was also the central moving force behind the Dundee Lunatic Asylum. By 1823 the agitation had been successful and the Linen Stamping Act was abolished.[28] While it is difficult to accurately account for the reasons behind the dramatic plunge in the Asylum's income, it is feasible that Edward Baxter's dealings with David Blair over the issue of linen stamping played a part in the decision of some of the original contributors to withdraw their support. Edward Baxter and his brothers appear never to have contributed to the funds of the Asylum although their support of the town's other charities was extensive. While Edward Baxter's father, William, and his uncle, John, had contributed to the Lunatic Asylum, by the beginning of the 1830s the financial support of the institution by the two senior Baxters had ended. By 1836, and the death of David Blair, all subscriptions to the Lunatic Asylum had ceased.

Thus the business conflict between Edward Baxter and David Blair may have spilled over into that of the charities which they supported. The central role of middle-class merchants in the organised charities of Dundee, in terms of both the financial support given by them *to* the charities and the civic prestige conferred on the merchants *by* the charities, meant that the relationship between the two was essentially symbiotic. Both parties gained from the association. There was no reason for a businessman to support a charity which he considered unprestigious for one reason or another; in this case Edward Baxter possibly chose not to support the Asylum because of its association with David Blair. The desire for group identification among the middle classes was a desire for identification with the most positive and important group. Edward Baxter and his brothers were relatively young men compared to David Blair, and Wm. Baxter & Son was becoming an increasingly important firm in the town. Therefore the more advantageous group with which to be associated was likely to have been the group which did not support the Lunatic Asylum, thus leading to a general drop in contributions to the institution.

Conflict was a regular feature of civic life in Dundee. The power struggles between the members of the Town Council and the Burgesses were often played out within the setting of the town's charitable institutions. Even though the Burgesses of the town were in theory represented by the Town Council, conflict between the two sections was manifest in the early years of the nineteenth century.[29] The Guildry records for 1818 asserted that:

> The Town Council for a period long past the memory of man,
> have not only kept the Burgesses in profound ignorance as to
> the management of the common good, but they have involved
> in equal darkness their administration of the affairs of the
> Hospital. And in place of supplying the funds to the support of
> decayed Burgesses, the Town Council as Managers of that
> charitable institution have been amassing large sums...and thus
> perverted the Hospital from its original destination.[30]

There were also calls for the accounts of those charities under the jurisdiction of the magistrates and town councils of the Scottish royal burghs to be audited, printed and published.[31]

David Blair and the Lunatic Asylum were also not strangers to conflict. In 1816 the Nine Trades refused to agree to the request for a loan from the managers of the Asylum,

> as they had already subscribed but had got no interest in the
> Asylum more than non-subscribers...and as they have no
> confidence in the self-elected managers, and will not therefore
> support institutions under the influence of the Magistrates or
> their creatures.[32]

A notice to this effect was inserted in the *Dundee Advertiser* where it was maintained that:

> the subscription paper...was the most absurd composition that had...been brought before the Trades. It purported to give security...but it was a declaration of the subscribers only...The subscribers could not grant to themselves a bond over the Asylum, as that was not their property. Indeed, from the state in which the Asylum now is, - without a constitution, or a name in law, - it was doubtful whether any authority could at present grant a security over it....Therefore, the subscription-paper was either downright nonsense, or it concealed a job, - a wish, on the part of the principal managers of the Asylum, to relieve themselves from the debt...and they were to do this by parcelling...the debt on the public. There was no alternative; the paper had either this meaning, or no meaning at all.
>
> Were the claims of the Lunatic Asylum preferable - were its practical benefits likely to be superior - to those of other institutions already existing in the place? Or were David Blair and Ebenezer Anderson, Esquires, the men for whose relief the Nine Trades ought to take away the half-crowns and shillings a month from their starving poor? No, David Blair, Esq. of Cookston, had always treated the Trades with contempt, except when he wished to obtain money from them. He had set his face with the greatest bitterness against public-spirit and the rights of the people of Dundee.[33]

The rights of the insane of the town and district appear to have become somewhat lost in the vitriolic attack which the Trades launched against David Blair and Ebenezer Anderson. This situation was perhaps not improved when Alexander Riddoch, provost of Dundee's self-elected Town Council from 1788 until 1818, came to Blair's aid in 1822 - only a few months before Riddoch's death. A deed of settlement was set up which arranged for £500 to be invested in heritable security, the interest of which was to be applied to the maintenance of 'such poor insane patients in the Lunatic Asylum near Dundee as should not have sufficient means to do so themselves'.[34] The overlapping civic and economic interests of Dundee's charitable elite meant that support for the town's charities depended as much, if not more, on the political and economic proclivities of the town's middle-class network as any other form of motivation.

Other problems could arise when individuals did not fulfil the roles expected of them. Involvement in the organised charities necessitated both a sense of commitment and responsibility, and part of the appeal of being offered the position of an office-bearer was the social status and trustworthiness which was implicitly conferred by the appointment. This trust was sometimes misplaced, however, as at least one of the Dundee charities, in addition to the Kirk Session, found to their cost. In 1837 a summons and action was raised in the Burgh Court of Dundee by several of the town's clergymen against one Charles R., tobacconist in Dundee and treasurer to the Kirk Session since 1833. Upon the treasurer's accounts being examined it had been found 'that he [Charles R.] had not kept them regularly or correctly', that there were 'considerable sums for which he has not properly accounted' and there 'remained a balance due by him to the said Kirksession [sic] of Four hundred and eighty five pounds five shillings and eleven pence halfpenny'. Requests made to him to repay the balance with interest had been rebuffed and it was noted that 'he...at least delayed so to do unless compelled'.[35] Charles R. was also treasurer of the Orphan Institution from around 1832-3 until 1837 when errors were discovered in his accounting and he was asked to produce an explanation and an adjustment of the accounts.[36]

Cases such as this - and there must have been many more - demonstrate the fragility of the infrastructure which the middle classes were attempting to create. Reliant on good and trustworthy individuals, the social and economic future of the town ultimately rested on the calibre of the men who stepped forward to assume positions of responsibility in the voluntary and civic organisations. Charles R. appears to have been accepted as one of those trustworthy individuals. William Norrie dedicates a substantial four pages to his biography in *Dundee Celebrities*. Only a brief paragraph refers to the aforementioned incident when Charles R. was the Kirk treasurer, noting discreetly that:

> in consequence, it is stated, of the malversation of a subordinate,
> in whom too much confidence had been placed, his [Charles
> R.'s] resignation had to be tendered.[37]

However, Charles R.'s legacy of poor accounting did not hinder his continued acceptance within Dundee society as in 1847 he was appointed secretary, librarian and treasurer to the Dundee Public Library 'after a keen contest'.[38]

By mid-century there was a general movement towards greater individual charitable activity amongst the larger benefactors, with several philanthropic ventures founded and funded by individual donors, many of whom were successful merchants in the town. The results of this 'new' individualistic philanthropy included the Molison

Hospital, established in the East Poorhouse in 1861 by Francis Molison (export merchant, Chairman of the Dundee Parochial Board from 1856-1872 and, incidentally, brother-in-law to Edward and David Baxter) at an expense to himself of more than £800.[39] Further philanthropic gestures from Molison included the establishment of an educational and industrial training facility for the blind at Dallfield House at a cost of more than £1,500.[40]

Many of these charitable gestures assumed an overtly paternalistic expression which was perhaps not out of keeping with the position of these new philanthropists who were often large-scale industrialists or politicians. Baxter Park was gifted:

> in grateful acknowledgement of the worldly means bestowed
> on us by a kind Providence...affording to the working population
> the means of relaxation and enjoyment after their hard labour
> and honest industry.[41]

This was followed by a similar gesture made in the 1890s by the Cox family, who owned another important textile manufacturing firm based in Lochee. Philanthropic foundations from the Cox family included a public swimming baths in 1895 and a public library in 1896.[42] Many of the grand charitable gestures of the second half of the nineteenth century were aimed at providing leisure facilities for the working classes - a new concept in philanthropy.

This kind of charitable activity closely resembled the mortified funds of the town's mercantile elite of the sixteenth, seventeenth and eighteenth centuries or the more traditional paternalistic gestures of the landed aristocracy, than the group-sponsored middle-class activity of the first half of the nineteenth century. What these philanthropic acts were most representative of, however, were the extensive fortunes carved out by the leading industrialists in the later half of the nineteenth century in conjunction with a growing personal confidence of their place in the community. Although these men formed a very exclusive and limited group of elite individuals, the impact made upon the city by their personal status and wealth was far-reaching. By the second half of the nineteenth century several of Dundee's textile manufacturing families had amassed considerable fortunes. The Cox family featured no less than five times in the list of the top ten estates confirmed in Scotland per annum between 1876 and 1913, leaving amounts that ranged from £218,499 (George Addison Cox, textile manufacturer and landowner) to £435,792 (Thomas Hunter Cox, linen merchant and manufacturer), while Sir David Baxter left £1,200,000 when he died in 1872.[43]

Notes

[1] DARC, GD/AY/7/1/2, DROI, Minute Book, 6 February 1833.

[2] *Dundee Advertiser*, 9 June 1815.

[3] *Dundee in 1793 and 1833*, 46.

[4] See Walsh, 'The Development of Organised Charity', 57.

[5] DARC, GD/AY/7/1/1, DROI, Minute Book, 1815-1823, 13 September, 4 November 1819.

[6] *Dundee Advertiser*, 31 March 1815.

[7] *Report of The Home* (1849).

[8] DARC, GD/AY/7/3/1, DROI, Register of Donations 1815-1949; DARC, *Handbook*.

[9] G. Douglas and G. Dalhousie Ramsay (eds.), *The Panmure Papers* (London, MCMVIII), 6-7.

[10] LS, Lamb and Millar, *Annals of Dundee*, 12 October 1838.

[11] DUA, THB 1/2/2, DRI, *Annual Report* (1839).

[12] A.H. Millar, *Glimpses of Old Dundee* (Dundee, 1925), 40.

[13] Angus Archives, MS 36, Minute Book of Brechin Dispensary, 1823-70.

[14] Angus Archives, MS 187/2, Brechin Mechanics' Institute, 34, 119-20, 147.

[15] *Report of the Home* (1849).

[16] LS, Pamphlets D4485 Dundee Royal Lunatic Asylum [DRLA], *Annual Report* (1822).

[17] A.J. Cooke (ed.), *Baxter's of Dundee* (Dundee, 1980).

[18] LS, L.Coll. 105(11), DCMA, *Annual Report* (1840).

[19] LS, L.Coll. 105(8), DCMA, *Annual Report* (1837).

[20] LS, L.Coll. 105(17), DCMA, *Annual Report* (1847).

[21] Edward Baxter himself, his father William Baxter, his sister and three brothers, David, John Gorrill and William Gorrill and two other Misses Baxter residing at the family home of Ellangowan.

[22] LS, L.Coll. 105(17), DCMA, *Annual Report* (1847).

[23] *Ibid.*

[24] See, for example, a donation of over four pounds in 1842, one pound and three shillings in 1843 and one pound and ten shillings in 1844. LS, L.Coll. 105(13-15), DCMA, *Annual Reports* (1842-44).

[25] LS, L.Coll. 105(16), DCMA, *Annual Report* (1845).

[26] LS, L.Coll. 434(11), DRLA, *Annual Report* (1824).

[27] Although the level of contributions to the Asylum fluctuated over the following years, subscriptions had dried up completely by the mid-1830s.

[28] Norrie, *Dundee Celebrities*, 369-370.

[29] A.J. Warden, *Burgh Laws of Dundee* (London, 1872), 106.

[30] DARC, GD/GRW/G 1/4, Sederunt of the Guildry of Dundee, 1776-1818.

[31] *Ibid.*

[32] Warden, *Burgh Laws*, 303.

[33] *Dundee Advertiser*, 22 November 1816.

[34] A.H. Millar (ed.), *Roll of Eminent Burgesses* (1887), 226-7.

[35] DARC, CH2/1218/69, General Session Records.

[36] DARC, GD/AY/7/1/2, DROI, Minute Book, 1830-46, 6 February 1833, 6 December 1837.

[37] Norrie, *Dundee Celebrities*, 255.

[38] Norrie, *Dundee Celebrities*, 256.

[39] LS, L.Coll. Box 398, 'Biographical Details'.

[40] Millar, *Roll of Eminent Burgesses*, 277.

[41] DUA, MS 105, Minute Book of the Baxter Park, No.1.

[42] DUA, MS 66, Cox Bros. Collection.

[43] R. Britton, 'Wealthy Scots, 1876-1913', *Bulletin of the Institute for Historical Research*, LVIII (1985), 78-94; A. Cooke, 'Baxter Brothers in Dundee', in Cooke, *Baxter's*, 20.

Chapter 5

Women and working men

'They deeply regret that they cannot regard all the Pensioners as of the excellent of the earth'.[1]

Not all of the Dundee charities directly relied upon business connections, as some of them were organised and run by women, including the Female Society, the Infant Schools Society and The Home. The Dundee Female Society was one of the earliest organised charities in Dundee to feature an all-female committee. Founded in 1804, the result of 'A few female friends...pitying' the situation of 'aged and indigent women' in Dundee, it was a charity which was run for and run by women and which was particularly anxious to receive assistance from the ladies of the town.[2] The object of the organisation was to assist those elderly women who were prevented from earning and who found themselves in temporary distress. The way in which the charity was run was not dissimilar to the way in which the Kirk Session's poor roll was managed, excepting the involvement of the female office-bearers and committee members. 'Pensioners' were accepted on to the Society's roll only after they had been visited and approved and a place was available for them. Prior to acceptance by the charity an individual's 'character and circumstances [were] to be inquired into', claimants had to have been resident in Dundee for three years and had also to already have their name on the roll of the Kirk Session, except in particular circumstances, while definitely no beggars were to 'have the benefit of the Society'.[3]

The Female Society provided a good example of a charity which straddled the bridge between individualistic philanthropy, based largely on religious precepts, and charity directed through the secular framework of an organised society. The Female Society also demonstrated how many of these early charities, aimed at alleviating dire poverty, were simply one step removed from the work of the established Kirk. The supporters of the charity were exhorted to 'view themselves as stewards for God' and to consider themselves accountable to Him for the manner in which they disposed of their wealth.[4] The charity assured its supporters that the Society's visitors, or dispensers of the charity, were regarded 'as the friend[s] of the solitary female' whose visits ensured that the supporters' charity was 'not abused'.[5] The annual report of 1837 expressed the hope that 'a mutual feeling exists', between the visitor and the pensioner, 'of thankfulness in receiving, and of blessedness in being permitted to give'.[6] Expressions of gratitude from the recipients of the charity were also recorded in the Society's literature. In the annual report of 1830 'a very pleasing instance of…gratitude' was noted when a poor widow, sometime 'object' of the charity, willed all her worldly goods to the Female Society.[7]

Despite its continuation throughout the nineteenth century the expression of charity dispensed by the Female Society continued to be rooted much more firmly in the eighteenth-century tradition of personal almsgiving. For example, the supporters of the charity vicariously took part in the physical act of dispensing charity through the activity of the visitors or 'almoners', more so than the anonymous form of philanthropy which would later come to be associated with nineteenth-century organised charity. As late as 1849 the Society described its activity as that of being 'almoners of the public'.[8] The continuing popularity of the charity no doubt partially lay in the preservation of the alms-giving system, its religious appeal particularly directed at Christian women as the traditional dispensers of philanthropy. The Society was not without its concessions to organised charity, however, as it was after all dealing with the urban, and thus increasingly more isolated, poor. The Female Society was able to blend a mixture of the old and new philanthropic traditions for the benefit of its supporters. Only those recommending individuals for the support of the Society, or those actually dispensing the relief, had any real contact with the recipients. The remainder of the supporters could enjoy the status of being charitable without incurring any of the possible dangers and probable unpleasantness of dealing with the poor face-to-face.

Nonetheless, the fact that some women were prepared to become visitors and to enter the homes of the urban poor makes them all the more striking as examples of active philanthropists of the period. In 1833-34 the Society boasted twenty-six visitors, half of whom were single women and half were married women.[9] This number had risen to thirty-seven by 1849, with a much greater preponderance of single than married women.[10] This amount of visitors compared favourably to that of the male missionaries employed by the Dundee City Mission Association, which was consistently below ten throughout this period.[11] Although the work involved was not exactly the same - the members of the Female Society visited only women and the primary concern of the city missionary was to provide moral rather than financial aid - it is surprising that no women were engaged by the City Mission. The Female Society's visitors were as well versed in supplying Bibles and religious tracts as they were in providing alms.

Little information survives concerning the members of the Female Society prior to 1833 as annual reports were not published by the charity before 1828 and no lists of office-bearers (or subscribers) were provided in the annual reports of the Society until 1832.[12] The committees appear to have been relatively small and informal, without a figurehead in the shape of a president, patroness or chairman and the office-bearers apparently limited to a treasurer and secretaries. The Clothing Society, another female-run venture about which little information remains, also followed a similar organisational structure. What can be discerned, however, was that the two societies appear to have been similar not only in their organisational structure but also in the actual office-bearers themselves. In 1833-4 a Mrs Jaffray, a clergyman's wife, was treasurer to the Female Society and one of the two treasurers of the Clothing Society, while a Mrs Rowell was one of the two secretaries of the Female Society in addition to holding the position of the second treasurer of the Clothing Society.[13] The longevity of charities such as the Female Society was partly due to their small and thus manageable size and possibly also partly due to the fact that they were 'female societies' in all respects, dealing only with the female poor and employing only women as office-bearers. The absence of men in the Society's organisation may have ensured the maintenance of the status quo.

Women involved in female-led charities could be found in most of the organisational roles, including that of treasurer, although this was often not the case outwith Scotland. A study of women's involvement in Irish charities has suggested that the relative absence of female treasurers might have been due to their legal status and the possible danger of the charitable funds falling into the hands of unscrupulous male relatives.[14] The legal position in Scotland was that a married woman could be nominated as a trustee only with the consent of her husband who was then liable for her conduct.[15] This situation suggests that men and women were working together in charitable ventures, even where the charities appeared to be ostensibly male-led or female-led. When the all-female committee of the Infant Schools Society purchased a house and land for a new school building, the trustees for the property, and the 'security for whatever money the Committee required beyond the sum raised', were all male.[16] Several of these gentlemen were related to members of the Society's committee and the remainder were subscribers.[17]

The need to involve men in female-run organisations was felt by other charities at particular stages in their development. While the charities remained small-scale the ladies appeared confident in their ability to manage their own affairs. Previous to large donations being received by the Dundee and District Rescue Home with a view to securing new premises,

> the Ladies' Committee had...borne the responsibility of the
> work, but for such an extended effort it was considered needful

to have the counsel and support of gentlemen who knew business.[18]

However, women played a significant, although far from commanding, role in the management of the town's Orphan Institution, and as it was a predominantly male-organised charity this was somewhat unusual. In the other larger Dundee charities where men dominated the organisational affairs, such as the Infirmary and the Lunatic Asylum, women were not involved on committee bodies. While not present at the original meetings held to discuss the establishment of the charity, women were present on the Board of the Orphan Institution as 'assistants' to the patroness from its opening in 1815 and by 1817 their role had developed into that of directors.[19] (Although not recorded as founding members, a possible 'silent' influence, which the women may have exerted over their male relatives regarding the instigation of the plan for the Orphan Institution, should not be discounted.) From its inception the charity appointed both a patron and a patroness. When honorary and extraordinary directors were appointed in 1817, in addition to the ordinary directors, these new directorships were given to both men and women, but rather than being representative of independent selection they largely reflected a familial connection. Out of the eight men and eight women who were elected to extraordinary directorships in 1817, there were six couples with a familial connection: James Guthrie, Esq. and Mrs Guthrie of Craigie; Graham Bower, Esq. and Mrs Bower of Kincaldrum; General and Mrs McKenzie of Broughty Ferry; Captain and Mrs McKenzie of Annfield; Rev. Dr Nicol and Mrs Nicol of Mains; and Thomas Erskine, Esq. and Miss Erskine of Linlathen. The remaining directorships went to a Mrs Mill of Annfield, a Miss Stirling of Dentroon, Captain Duncan and a David Arkley, Esq. of Clepington.[20]

The high incidence of familial relationship suggests that the new directors were often solicited as a 'couple'. This connection may be responsible for the more positive role which women assumed in the male-led Orphan Institution. However, were they simply adjuncts to their male relatives or was it their involvement which drew in the men? Women's influence in the active management of the charity appears to have decreased over time from the high level of involvement of the early years. From at least as early as 1830 women appear to have been excluded from committee meetings. By the 1840s the women involved with the Orphan Institution were no longer noted as directors in the annual reports but as 'Lady Visitors' or 'Lady Governesses'.[21] Prior to the 1830s women had been very actively involved in the charity through the solicitation and collection of subscriptions. Their new titles may have been as much a reflection of the mores of contemporary society, which frowned upon women taking such active roles, as the abilities or usefulness of the women themselves. Furthermore, this exclusion of women fits neatly with the ethos of the charity which was highly concerned to maintain and reaffirm rigid roles for members of society.

Women's traditional role as dispensers of charity had not included the solicitation of funds from strangers on a regular and organised basis. The ethos of the Orphan Institution could have controlled the level of involvement of the middle-class female membership as much as it attempted to control the lives of the working-class recipients of its charity. This control does appear to have been resisted, however, as by 1836 the female contingent of the Institution was anxious to again become more involved in the affairs of the charity. A Mrs Boyack expressed her anxiety to promote the interests of the Institution and volunteered her services to obtain subscriptions, and as a result it was decided that each of the directors and lady visitors were to be provided with subscription papers and were asked to provide 'their best exertions to obtain additional subscriptions'.[22] By 1845 there was the suggestion that the propriety of convening the lady visitors 'from time to time to manage the affairs of the House' should be considered, indicating an apparent willingness to include women in the running of the Institution again.[23]

By the second half of the nineteenth century, women were also assuming the role of major charitable benefactors in Dundee. Funds from the late Mrs William Curr plus a donation from the estate of the late Mrs Francis Molison went to support the building of a new institution in Lochee for the Rescue Home.[24] Funds from Mrs Molison also supported the building of the new Institute for the Blind in Magdalen Green.[25] Mary Ann Baxter and her leading role in the establishment of University College provide a further example. The majority of these women were either the spouse of, or related to, major charitable male benefactors in the town but the original impetus for the charitable deeds of the men could have lain as much with the prompting of their female relatives as with their own consciences.

In some areas, however, the female contribution to the Dundee charities appears somewhat restricted. An historian of organised charity in England has noted the importance of the bazaar, essentially a female enterprise, to charity fund-raising. The rise in popularity of charity bazaars in England dates from the 1820s.[26] However the incidence of these events, at least in the early years of the nineteenth century, appears to have been remarkably low in Dundee. A sale of ladies' work was held in aid of the Clothing and Indigent Sick Societies in 1827 and in 1831 a similar event was held in aid of the Infirmary and the Infant Schools. Although the funds they raised were not inconsiderable - over £255 and £356 respectively - these appear to have been isolated incidents.[27] The object of the ladies who proposed the sale on behalf of the Infant Schools 'was to relieve them[selves] from debt unavoidably incurred at the commencement [of the charity]', indicating that the sale was seen as a necessary means to an end rather than as a forerunner to a regular system of fund-raising.[28] A suggestion that the ladies might like to hold a similar event on behalf of the Lunatic Asylum came to nothing.[29]

A study of English charitable society reports indicates that 'thousands of small sales did not reach the newspapers, but were announced simply by word of mouth, or by a notice on a church or chapel door'.[30] The reports of the charitable organisations of Dundee, and their annual statement of accounts, are silent in this respect. As it is unlikely that the managers of the charities would have overlooked the opportunity to encourage different methods of raising funds by mentioning them in their annual reports it appears probable that the bazaar was not a popular method of fund-raising in Dundee, at least for the first half of the century, or that there were not enough women willing to organise such events. It has been suggested that 'where women played a role in a charity bazaars were likely to follow'.[31] However, this was evidently not the case in Dundee and it raises implications for the role which women envisaged for themselves in the town's charities.

'It is pleasing to record that one of its most liberal benefactors has been a working man'[32]

While charities were anxious to receive contributions from all sections of society the methods employed to raise funds and attract subscribers, while broadly similar to all the charities, were not equally accessible to all social groups. Many of the working classes may have found themselves excluded from the opportunity to listen to charity sermons, and thus excluded from becoming contributors, through the practice of pew renting.[33] This could be compounded by ideas advanced by charities themselves as they attempted to maximise the funds raised through charity sermons. The Orphan Institution, for example, actively considered the idea of appointing officials at the church doors when their annual charity sermon was taking place and who would be instructed to only allow admittance to those whom they considered to be contributors with a generous spirit.[34]

Nonetheless, the working-class charitable impulse was considered by nineteenth-century contemporaries, and also by some twentieth-century historians, to have been of no little importance. The Rev. Robert Small, commenting on the 'common people' of late eighteenth-century Dundee, noted that 'the proportion they bestow, in all charitable contributions, at least equals, if not exceeds, that of their superiors in opulence'.[35] The working classes were certainly encouraged to become contributors.

Thomas Chalmers' support for the 'penny-a-week' subscriptions of the lower classes was rooted in the belief that the poor would be less inclined to allow themselves to slip into pauperism 'on the high ground of being a dispenser of charity' coupled with the idea that 'before he can submit to become a recipient of charity, he must let himself farther down than a poor man in ordinary circumstances'.[36] This is a different argument to that employed in Dundee by both the Society for Relief of the Indigent Sick and the Infirmary; the labouring classes were encouraged to become contributors in order to provide for themselves in case of future need as much as to attain the status of the benevolent.

The argument advanced by the Infirmary appears to have had the stronger appeal to the working classes in Dundee as it was the only one of the town's charities to enjoy a relatively high and sustained level of working-class support. There were few examples of regular working-class contributions to the other charities in the town. It could be argued that none of the Dundee charities, apart from the Infirmary and the Society for Relief of the Indigent Sick, positively sought out working-class contributions, although such funds were eagerly received by all the charitable organisations in the town. The tone and substance of many annual reports, perhaps the most widely used fund-raising tool of the charities, was aimed squarely at the middle classes and their content discussed the poor or working classes in an overtly patronising manner.[37] It is evident that this would have had little positive effect in encouraging contributions from the working classes themselves. The Infirmary reports, meanwhile, targeted workers as prospective contributors and, although still somewhat patronising in tone, the appeal of the institution was its emphasis on the self-help nature of the worker's contribution rather than the charity which would be received.[38] Essentially, the Infirmary appealed to the working classes on the principle of 'self-help', but an element of fear was also employed. The prospect of possible death or disability on the part of the breadwinner and resulting destitution for the family was a very real concern.

Contributors to the Infirmary represented a very broad spectrum of the town's working classes, including a high percentage of skilled workers. Textile workers, harbour porters and dock workers, contractors and employees of the Dundee Water Works and Gas Company, railway and tram workers, and workmen employed at various occupations including brass founding, plastering, furniture making, brushmaking, photography and newspaper publishing were all contributors to the Infirmary at some point over the nineteenth century.[39] Well-known Dundee employers such as Keiller's Confectionery and Chocolate Works, the *Dundee Advertiser* and Valentine and Son Photographic Publishers also featured in the lists of contributing workplaces, although the largest single collections originated with the large textile employers. In 1875 over £80 was collected by the employees of the Gilroy Brothers' Tay Works, more than £110 from the Baxter Brothers' employees, and over £200 from the workers at Cox Brothers' Camperdown Linen Works in Lochee.[40] These figures were far in excess of the other collections raised in that year and the sum total raised by the textile workers, of almost £400, comprised between a fifth and a quarter of the monies raised from collections made for the Dundee Royal in public works in 1875.[41]

While it remains impossible to ascertain the origins of every working-class contribution made to the Infirmary, nonetheless, it is evident that many workers were themselves initiating collections. In 1829 it was noted that 'work-people [were] contributing of their wages, and even forming societies for the same excellent purpose', while in 1865 the workmen from the Monifieth foundry donated the proceeds of their 'Annual Soiree' to the Dundee Infirmary.[42] While employers had an important role in encouraging and in organising contributions, once the system was in place the working classes continued to lend it their support. From as early as 1831 it was announced in the Infirmary's annual report that in order to encourage working-class contributions, arrangements could be made by which weekly voluntary contributions 'not exceeding a penny a week from any one individual' could be collected at the different manufactories.[43] This idea also provided for a regular system of contributions protected against trade fluctuations, which often had a marked effect on workplace donations.[44] Furthermore, it was announced that:

> The workpeople who contribute among themselves to the
> requisite amount, to be permitted to elect from their number,
> persons to be entitled to the privileges of Governors [with the
> ability to recommend patients] for the year.[45]

Examples of workmen recommending individuals to the Dundee Royal included 'the workers at Craigie Mill', who featured several times at mid-century. Similarly, recommendations came from 'Robert Turnbull for the Claverhouse Workers', including one for a female who was recorded not as an employee but as a housewife, thus demonstrating how the benefits of workplace subscriptions could be extended to provide medical care for workers' dependents.[46]

By the end of the nineteenth century the importance of working-class contributions to the income of the Dundee Infirmary was crucial. The institution never publicly acknowledged this fact yet, when working-class contributions had been less than middle-class subscriptions some gestures of thanks had been made to the workmen. The 'numerous and handsome contributions' of the working classes were acknowledged 'with pleasure' in the annual report of 1846.[47] However, as the value of the workplace contributions increased compared to middle-class subscriptions the directors paid correspondingly less attention to the workers' contributions in the annual reports. Previously listed within the accounts in second place to subscriptions, workplace contributions dropped to fourth place in 1892, following on from 'contributions of less than twenty-one shillings' (£11 in total) and 'church collections' (£644 in total). This was despite the fact that collections from public works in 1892 had reached £2,390.[48]

Other working-class fund-raising activities, such as Hospital Saturday, also failed to merit any attention from the directors in their annual reports. This method of raising funds involved street collections as well as workplace contributions and was a nation-wide fund-raising event under the control of working men. In return for the funds raised and donated to a particular institution the men received a number of subscribers' letters, which were then distributed to workers in need. Hospital Saturdays raised almost £280 over two years for the benefit of the Dundee Infirmary.[49] Nonetheless, no mention of the events or of the monies raised was made in any part of the institution's annual reports other than their inclusion in a general list of 'larger' donations.

The Infirmary perhaps frowned upon the linking of its name with these street-based activities. While the institution was pleased to identify with genteel middle-class fund-raising activities, such as sermons and public lectures, there appears to have been a reluctance to embrace the methods employed by the working classes. This situation can be contrasted with that at Aberdeen where the 1899 Infirmary Annual Report noted that the Hospital Saturday Fund had displayed 'great activity' and had succeeded in maintaining the level of 'their former handsome contribution of £600' for which the directors tendered their 'grateful acknowledgements'.[50]

A small but notable number of working-class contributions were directed towards the other charities in the town. A 'miscellaneous' category of contributions to the Industrial Schools Society included a donation of one pound, plus the proceeds of the sale of a watch which came to over two pounds 'from a working man, saved from whisky and tobacco'; one pound from the 'Servants of Blackie & Son, Glasgow'; one pound and six shillings from the servants in the Lunatic Asylum; and seven shillings from the Dundee Young Men's Yearly Society.[51] Although only comprising an extremely small part of total contributions, these sums were highly significant in terms of the overall level of working-class contributions that were made to the Dundee charities, excluding the Infirmary, as a whole.

The activities of the benevolent in Dundee - regardless of their conscious or unconscious motives - shaped and directed much of the social and economic infrastructure of the town. The decisions made by individuals as to how to dispose of their income had a significant impact on the way in which the town developed. The townscape was shaped by philanthropic gestures such as the founding of public parks, while the charitable activities of prominent individuals on behalf of the town and its community were recognised in bricks and mortar. Although the upper and working classes did have a role to play as contributors it was the middle classes who remained central to the viability of the organised charities of Dundee - and who strived to maintain that importance and the accompanying power and influence in the town.

Notes

[1] LS, Pamphlets D4487I, DFS, *Annual Report* (1834).

[2] *Dundee Advertiser*, 14 December 1804.

[3] LS, Pamphlets D4487I, DFS, *Annual Report* (1834).

[4] *Ibid.*

[5] LS, Pamphlets D4487I, DFS, *Annual Report* (1833).

[6] LS, L.Coll. 55(13), DFS, *Annual Report* (1837).

[7] DFS, *Annual Report* (1830).

[8] LS, L.Coll. 55(13) DFS, *Annual Report* (1849).

[9] The women were listed as 'committee and visitors' therefore it is assumed that all twenty-six women were involved in both capacities.

[10] LS, L.Coll. 55(13), DFS, *Annual Report* (1849).

[11] The missionaries were paid for the work they carried out for the City Mission Association.

[12] Limited information can be gleaned from the Dundee Directories. In 1817-18, a Mrs Geddes was the treasurer of the Female Society and a Miss Stephens the secretary. *Dundee Directory 1817-18.*

[13] *Dundee Directory 1833-4.*

[14] M. Luddy, *Women and Philanthropy in Nineteenth-Century Ireland* (Cambridge, 1995), 177.

[15] A.J.P. Menzies, *The Law of Scotland affecting Trustees* (Edinburgh, 1913), 51, 53. I am grateful to Chris Davey and members of the Faculty of Law at the University of Dundee for this reference.

[16] Alexander Balfour, Patrick Scott, John Symers, John Boyd Baxter, W.G. Baxter and Robert Gray.

[17] Messrs. Balfour, Scott and Boyd Baxter were presumably the husbands of Mrs Balfour, Mrs Scott, and Mrs Boyd Baxter, all committee members, while W.G. Baxter and Robert Gray were subscribers. A Miss Baxter and a Miss Gray were also committee members, suggesting that a familial link also existed between Baxter and Gray and members of the committee. A Mr Symers was also a subscriber. LS, L.Coll. 213(10), *Report of the Committee of the Greenfield and Wallace Feus Infant Schools* (1836).

[18] *Dundee Year Book 1883.*

[19] DARC, GD/AY/7/1/1, DROI, Minute Book, 1815-23.

[20] It is impossible to ascertain the exact relationship of the couples from the annual report itself, but working with information from other charitable subscription lists it is reasonable to assume that they were either husband and wife or father and daughter.

[21] DARC, GD/DO1/5/1, DROI, Directors Reports, 1830-1919, *Annual Report* (1839, 1844).

[22] DARC, GD/AY/7/1/2, DROI, Minute Book, 1830-46, 4 May 1836.

[23] DARC, GD/AY/7/1/2, DROI, Minute Book, 1830-46, 15 March 1845.

[24] *Dundee Year Book 1883.*

[25] *Dundee Year Book 1885.*

[26] F.K. Prochaska, *Women and Philanthropy in 19th Century England* (Oxford, 1980), 50.

[27] LS, Lamb and Millar, *Annals of Dundee*, 301, 35. The sale of 1827 was of sufficient rarity value for Lamb to comment that it was the first notice of a bazaar that he had come across.

[28] LS, L.Coll. 213(9A), *Report of the Committee of the Dundee Infant Schools* (1831).

[29] LS, L.Coll. 434(17), DRI, *Annual Report* (1832).

[30] Prochaska, *Women and Philanthropy*, 53.

[31] Prochaska, *Women and Philanthropy,* 57.

[32] DARC, *Handbook.*

[33] C.G. Brown, 'The Costs of Pew-renting: Church management, church-going, and social class in nineteenth-century Glasgow', *Journal of Ecclesiastical History*, Vol. 38, 3 (1987), 347-361.

[34] See, for example, DARC, GD/AY/7/1/1, DROI, Minute Book, 1815-23, 13 September 1819.

[35] *Dundee in 1793 and 1833*, 47.

[36] S.J. Brown, *Thomas Chalmers and the Godly Commonwealth in Scotland* (Oxford, 1982), 67.

[37] See, for example, the *Annual Reports* of the DFS.

[38] See, for example, DRI, *Annual Report* (1831).

[39] See, for example, the *Annual Reports* of the DRI for 1865, 1870, 1875, 1895 and 1900. DUA, THB1/2/4-6a.

[40] DUA, THB 1/2/5, DRI, *Annual Report* (1875).

[41] *Ibid.*

[42] LS, L.Coll. 404(1), DRI, *Annual Report* (1829); DUA, THB 1/2/4, DRI, *Annual Report* (1865).

[43] LS, L.Coll. 404(1), DRI, *Annual Report* (1831).

[44] See, for example, DUA, THB 1/2/6, DRI, *Annual Reports* (1886-7); Greater Glasgow Health Board Archive, HB14/2/9, *Glasgow Royal Infirmary Annual Reports 1883-1894* (1884).

[45] LS, L.Coll. 404(1), DRI, *Annual Report* (1831).

[46] DUA, THB 1/5/2, DRI, Admissions and Discharge Register 1848-58.

[47] DUA, THB 1/2/2, DRI, *Annual Report* (1846).

[48] DUA, THB 1/2/6, DRI, *Annual Report* (1892).

[49] DUA, THB 1/2/6a, DRI, *Annual Report* (1900).

[50] Aberdeen University Archives, Lper Aa L1.3 AIr, Aberdeen Royal Infirmary, *Annual Report* (1899).

[51] LS, L.Coll. 41(2), DISS, *Annual Report* (1847).

Chapter 6

The Impact of Charity on Dundee

'The object of this Society is not to check benevolence, but to assist the Public in directing it
into channels where good may result instead of evil.'[1]

While Dundee had much in common with the other major nineteenth-century Scottish
towns, each of those towns was unique in its pattern of development due to specific
local conditions, minimal state intervention and the importance of individual
enterprise. The ability to mould and shape the infrastructure of a town in the
nineteenth century was available to the urban middle classes through the vehicle of
philanthropy. However, the inclinations and sensibilities of the middle classes in
Dundee shaped the town as much by the organisations they decided not to support
as by those institutions which they did advocate.

Charities that aimed to help women were particularly poorly represented in
Dundee. This appears a curious omission in the 'woman's town', with the absence
of a lying-in hospital being a particularly striking feature. The number of women
whose children were delivered by the Infirmary was very small in relation to the
size of the community and the number of young female incomers to the town. From
the opening of the Infirmary up to mid-century the number of women delivered by
the institution per annum never exceeded fifty-three (1843) and was as low as one
(1826).[2] Meanwhile the dispensary at the much smaller town of Perth - which had
as one of its objectives the 'delivery of poor pregnant women' - was able to record
forty-eight deliveries, including one case of twins, in 1835 and thirty-seven deliveries
the following year.[3]

In fact, the Dundee Infirmary went out of its way to exclude lying-in patients
from the charity. No midwife would be paid for lying-in women 'unless the patient
be recommended, and the recommendation lodged with the Apothecary'.[4]
Registration had to be 'eight days before the delivery' and would certainly have
precluded a number of women from gaining access.[5] However, it was not so unusual
for infirmaries of the period to exclude lying-in patients and as a result specialised
lying-in hospitals were established. What is striking in Dundee is that no specialised
institutional facilities for pregnant women were provided before the closing years
of the nineteenth century. Edinburgh and Glasgow had had maternity hospitals from

the end of the eighteenth century and by the late nineteenth century boasted several specialist hospitals for the treatment of female maladies, such as the Glasgow Hospital for Diseases Peculiar to Women.[6] Dundee, however, did not establish a specialist hospital for women until the opening of the Private Hospital for Women in 1896 which provided the opportunity for women to be treated by female practitioners. A maternity hospital was not opened until 1899, more than 100 years after similar institutions opened in Glasgow and Edinburgh. Furthermore, the new hospital did not result from individual philanthropy but from the initiative of the Forfar Medical Association which donated £10,000 for the venture.[7]

Rather than indicating a direct neglect of women's needs in Dundee, however, the lack of a maternity hospital may have been more the reflection of the powerful influence of the town's charitable middle classes. Specialist hospitals were as much the result of medical men's attempts to gain power and influence as any other cause. However, physicians and surgeons of the period needed the financial backing of public subscribers to enable them to open and operate new hospitals. Doctors who aimed to specialise in this early period were often viewed as outlandish. Furthermore, pregnancy and childbirth were highly sensitive issues for the pious middle classes, particularly when some of the women who found themselves in a delicate condition were also unmarried. If backing was not forthcoming the hospitals would not materialise.

Any subjects surrounding female sexuality - and its consequences - appear to have been ignored by the charitable Dundee middle classes. The Home's first report commented, somewhat coyly, on the 'wretched state of evil that exists in this town'.[8] If this was indeed how contemporaries viewed the situation then Dundee had been slow to deal with this 'evil'. Although the question of dealing with prostitutes appears not to have been a major pre-occupation of the charitable in Dundee before 1848 it would be naive to suppose that prostitution was not a fact of life, particularly in view of Dundee being a port and a barracks town as well as a major urban centre. The Dundee City Mission had been raising awareness of the prevalence of prostitution since at least the late 1830s, while a private House of Refuge was reported by the *Dundee Advertiser* to have opened in 1844.[9]

The town's middle classes had largely shied clear of the subject of prostitution and the possible establishment of a Magdalene asylum in Dundee. It was only with the involvement of the upper classes and Lady Jane Ogilvy that a notable refuge for 'fallen women' was realised. The first annual report of The Home commented that the 'number of the applications for admission is a sufficient proof of the great necessity of such an Institution in Dundee'; in fact the charity had received more applications than it had room to deal with and plans were already underway in 1849 to extend the Paton's Lane building.[10] The thirty-five admissions over the first year would barely have affected the number of prostitutes in the city, which was considered to have stood at several hundred in the late 1830s.[11] As was frequently the case with the other charitable institutions in the town, the implementation of an institutional policy dependent upon voluntary support meant that only a limited number of recipients could be provided for.

Further moves towards reforming the 'fallen' women of Dundee continued to be small-scale. It took the arrival of one Miss Heriot-Maitland from Edinburgh before another venue was opened in the town for the reception of prostitutes. The Dundee and District Rescue Home was established in 1878, in Milnbank Road, with the dual aims to both prevent crime and reclaim women who were 'proving at once a plague and disgrace'.[12] The establishment of such a new institution was indeed a real gesture of charity as it was noted at the time that since the death of Lady Ogilvy, the original 'Home' had become more of a penitentiary than a home and reformatory.[13] The Rescue Home was to employ only 'moral suasion' in its efforts to train up the 'fallen' women into suitable servants, several of whom would be found positions overseas in America, South Africa and Australia.[14]

However, the very limited facilities available for the reception of prostitutes in Dundee had a correspondingly negligible impact upon their numbers in the town. While the committee of The Home in Paton's Lane urged persons in need of servants to apply to the institution, the number of inmates which were successfully placed remained relatively small. In 1849, out of thirty-five admissions over the year, twenty-three women remained in the house, five had left of their own volition, three had been 'returned to friends', one had been expelled and only three had 'gone to service.'[15] While it has to be considered that large institutional Magdalene asylums in Glasgow and Edinburgh would also have served a limited number, it is the lack of public initiative and support for such an institution which was the serious deficiency in Dundee.

The lack of a Magdalene asylum, and the middle-class inhibitions and distaste which surrounded the whole subject of women's sexuality, also accounted for the absence of a Lock hospital in the town. In not founding such an institution, however, Dundee fell behind the other major Scottish towns in terms of charitable provision and also in the development of medical expertise. Glasgow's Lock hospital had existed since 1805 and by the 1870s it had become the largest specialist hospital in Scotland, continuing to receive patients up until the Second World War. A Lock hospital was founded in Edinburgh in 1835 and although it closed in 1847, with patients returning to the Royal Infirmary for treatment, the notable list of subscribers indicated a well-supported institution.[16]

The reluctance of the benevolent in Dundee to follow their counterparts in Glasgow, Edinburgh and Aberdeen in founding a lying-in hospital, Magdalene asylum and Lock hospital suggests something quite specific was at work in the minds of the middle classes. Dundee had, in the first half of the nineteenth century, developed a reputation as a dirty, overcrowded and unattractive place. The town's middle classes, who were working hard to create a more attractive and prosperous Dundee, would have been reluctant to attract further negative attention and comment. While clearly a policy of self-delusion, the absence of a formal institution for the reformation of prostitutes or a hospital for treating the results of that trade could give the impression that such facilities were not required in Dundee. Prostitution and its consequences were not an acknowledged problem in a town which was trying hard to clean up its image, both metaphorically and literally.

Control or coercion?

Other than as a way to help the disadvantaged there were of course many other - and perhaps central - reasons for the middle classes to contribute to charitable organisations. It has been argued that the 'flurry' of charitable activity of the early nineteenth century should be viewed not as 'the beginnings of a new philanthropic order' but rather as 'the attempt of conservatives...to hang on to a hierarchical social order of mutual obligation'.[17] Was the tradition of eighteenth-century paternalism transformed into nineteenth-century social control in the industrialising towns a result of middle-class fears or the influence of the new urban-industrialist philanthropists? An 'international association of paternalism and textiles' has been claimed, thus placing Dundee firmly within this association.[18] The apogee of paternalist behaviour has been identified as being between 1850 and 1875.[19] The most visible acts of the nineteenth-century Dundee philanthropists do fit this pattern, including the grand gestures made by the textile manufacturing Baxter and Cox families.

However, in addition to its manifestation in large-scale gestures, paternalism also embodied a sense of responsibility and duty.[20] In the early nineteenth century paternalism of this nature was notably absent in Dundee. Exceptions to this were perhaps demonstrated in the five factory schools that were established in the town by the late 1830s.[21] Any paternalist aspirations, however, which aimed to see the educational condition of the factory children improved were negated by the excessively long hours worked by the children before they reached the classroom and the subsequent effects this had on their ability to learn. Similarly, the textile manufacturers built few houses for their employees despite a dire shortage of decent housing, a situation possibly reflected in the establishment of the Model Lodging-House Association in 1849.[22] It was not until 1866-7 that Baxter's began to build houses for their workers.[23] It has been argued that this lack of employer-provided housing offered 'less scope for social control' than other textile-dominated areas such as New Lanark.[24] This is not to say, however, that the textile manufacturers in Dundee lacked control over their workers. The mill and factory owners effectively exercised such control over their employees during their hours of employment which, due to their considerable length, meant in reality that employers exerted control over almost all of their workers' waking hours.[25]

It is unclear where acts of nineteenth-century charity moved from being expressions of paternalism into a desire to enforce some form of social control, or if the two were ever entirely separate.[26] Subscribers who contributed to the Industrial Schools were probably genuinely concerned for the well-being and condition of the street children, but the motivation behind their contributions was also concerned with moral reform and a desire to reduce incidences of theft in the town; something which directly affected the subscribers' pockets. Supporters of the Orphan Institution wanted to help with the provision of education for disadvantaged children in Dundee, but they were also anxious to ensure that that education would be of a suitably restricted kind, aimed at fitting the working-class child for his or her future in the Dundee community as either an apprentice or a servant.

One of the greatest difficulties with any interpretation which views charitable activity from a social control perspective is the lack of support which many of these charities received from the larger community. The Dundee Lunatic Asylum was a case in point. Although it was a charity which dealt largely with lunatic paupers and with people who easily could have been perceived as dangerous or deviant and potentially in need of control, it was the least well supported of all the Dundee charities of this period. As the nineteenth century progressed, and the size of the population in the town and the number of lunatics in the Asylum increased, the number of contributions to the charity correspondingly decreased. By the mid-1830s the relative importance of charitable contributions to the Asylum, compared to funds raised through other channels, was minimal. Possible demonstrations of control over the insane were limited to the increasing role which the police commissioners played in the apprehension of alleged lunatics who were then sent to the Asylum, although this was as often as not accompanied by the commissioners' assumption of financial obligation for the individual, thus implying a more paternalist than controlling role.[27]

There were also few charities specifically aimed at certain social groups which may have been perceived as requiring some control. One observer, commenting on the Irish in Dundee in 1850, noted:

> Their vile slang and immoral habits have seriously injured the...character of the poor population of Dundee, and I think throughout Scotland. The low Irish are not a very improvable race. They cling to their rags, their faith and their filth with all the besottedness of perfect ignorance and stupidity.[28]

The Irish formed a social group which was clearly despised and perhaps feared by certain sections of mid-century society in Dundee, but there were no specific charitable organisations which aimed to control, modify or direct their behaviour. A feeling that they may not have accepted 'interference' from Protestant charities - or indeed that they were beyond such help - may have influenced the Dundee charitable community, although as has been seen the Irish regularly did receive the benefit of at least one of the town's charities, the Infirmary, to the extent that complaints were made that they were monopolising the institution.[29]

One aspect of the Infirmary's charitable system which could be interpreted as a potential form of social control was the scheme involving the recommendation of patients for admission to the institution. The privilege of recommendation was secured by the subscription of a stipulated sum which allowed the contributor to nominate a certain number of patients for treatment. However, the obligations involved in the recommendation of a patient would appear to have outweighed any supposed advantages relating to social control. The payment of weekly board had to be guaranteed for the patient and responsibility assumed in the event of his discharge or death. This assumption of responsibility reflected an outlook rooted much more firmly in paternalism than in any aspirations towards social control.

Nonetheless, there is little difficulty in identifying the charitable organisations of the period as *potential* vehicles for social control. Contributing to such organisations was often promoted as a way to avoid scenes of disorder and mayhem. With few means at their disposal to support law and order in the town, at least for the early years of the nineteenth century, placatory - often charitable - measures were an undeniably useful tool. The involvement of town authorities as officials and supporters of the organised charities demonstrated their approval of the institutions not only as good examples of civic action, but also as institutions which would help to 'keep the peace and reduce social costs'.[30] The Industrial Schools, which were largely funded by the Member of Parliament George Duncan, were a good example of such a system in mid nineteenth-century Dundee.

Any activities which were directed at the management of the poor need not be viewed simply as measures of coercion and control carried out in order to avoid trouble, but as a more subtle - and perhaps not fully conscious - means to influence the views of the poor and to reinforce the social role which they were expected to fulfil in society.[31] The role of relief measures as agencies of social control can best be viewed not in the light of one class attempting to dominate another, but of one class attempting to establish a form of social structure, which was felt to be lacking or under threat, on the nineteenth-century industrial town. Charities played a central role in this process. This influence can be identified in the Orphan Institution and The Home, but it was more a stabilising rather than an overtly repressive influence which intended to 'save' these individuals and reaffirm their correct societal roles. In the case of The Home and the Orphan Institution this was as competent servants for the middle classes.

As with many similar charities of the period, however, the activities of the Orphan Institution did not address the real source of their anxieties. The apparently ungovernable and rebellious lower strata or underclass of the poor which fuelled middle-class fears was never approached with assistance or instruction. It was only a select group of the children of the respectable working class which was targeted by the directors of the Orphan Institution, in order to prevent the children's dissolution into pauperism and anti-social behaviour. Furthermore, although the charity was imbued with a desire to inculcate middle-class values and mores into the children of the working classes, the relatively small numbers of children who received the attentions of the Institution meant that this attempt at 'social control' would always play a very minor part in the restructuring of the nineteenth-century urban community.

Essentially, these attempts at the manipulation of class roles did not result in the creation of a system of overt class control. Despite the fact that many of the leading figures in these organisations aimed to exert control over the working classes it is doubtful whether any such attempts could have been complete. The wide range of alternative ideologies available confounded any attempts at, and aspirations for, outright control.[32] The influence of the charities also affected only a limited section of the poor or the working classes, and only on a temporary basis, which meant that much of that influence or control was transitory. It is also not inconceivable that the working classes were able to play one charity off against another, particularly taking into account potential rivalries between philanthropists and their associations.[33] Possibly, the working classes were also able to take only what they wanted from the organisations and to ignore anything which they found unacceptable.[34] Over time, the middle-class 'mission' became one of 'civilising' rather than 'controlling' the working classes.[35]

Historians who are critical of the use of control theories in the explanation of philanthropic motivation often favour more simple explanations based largely on humanitarianism. F.K. Prochaska comments upon the 'recent trend among historians of Victorian Britain...to interpret charity as the means by which the dominant professional and commercial classes confirmed their power and status' and 'sought to "control" the poor', while he considers that it is 'suggestive to think of the history of philanthropy broadly as the history of kindness'.[36] The two theories should not be viewed as necessarily opposed or incompatible. All of the charitable foundations of the period benefited from a mixture of motivating factors. The drive behind the establishment of Britain's first foundling hospital in the eighteenth century had been as much 'mercantilist as well as humanitarian', in order to 'rescue young lives that would otherwise be wasted and render them useful to the state'.[37] Humanitarianism was undoubtedly an element of the philanthropic impulse of the period but it was often coupled with another motivating factor or precondition which acted as the determinant in transforming concern into action.[38] For the directors of the Orphan Institution, for example, a desire to shape or control the lives of the respectable orphan poor of Dundee provided that factor.

Philanthropy was also employed as a tool to augment the civic standing of the benefactors' hometown as much as the lives of its inhabitants. Through this form of charitable activity the role of the middle-class elite in the affairs of the town, and the importance of their role within social and economic activities, was strengthened. Civic pride thus provided a powerful motivation to contribute to organised charity. The institutional charitable organisations were of primary importance to this expression of civic pride, as was demonstrated by the involvement of the important civic bodies and officials in the town's major charities. The foundation of charities such as the Infirmary and the Lunatic Asylum provided an occasion for procession, pageantry and the promotion of Dundee. These occasions were also a way of demonstrating a form of civic paternalism towards the working classes through the establishment of public gala days to coincide with the occasion of annual general meetings, which in the early years of the century were often accompanied with much pomp and brilliance.

It was claimed that 'the numbers assembled to join and witness the procession' for the laying of the foundation stone of the Dundee Lunatic Asylum 'were never equalled in this town on any similar occasion'. A time capsule was inserted containing a glass bottle with coins, an almanac, two Dundee newspapers and a roll of appropriately inscribed parchment.[39] The town's penchant for processions decreased over the years however, in line with changing attitudes towards street behaviour. The last straw for the Infirmary came in 1818 when it was stated:

> That as the benefit resulting to the Infirmary from public processions, bears no proportion to the evils which the exhibitions produce, by occasioning idleness and dissipation and thereby injuring both the means and morals of the labouring classes…no procession shall in future be allowed.[40]

Charities could also provide civic support in rather more direct ways. In order to secure a good financial return, money bequeathed to a charity could be used to grant loans to individuals or to other organisations in the town. The ability of charitable organisations to lend out money in this way, and also to borrow money, was granted under a Charter of Incorporation. The Infirmary, the Lunatic Asylum and the Orphan Institution enjoyed the greater flexibility in financial affairs which incorporation brought to charitable organisations in this period. In addition to the 'hidden' financial benefits it also brought the cachet of being able to append the 'Royal' prefix to the organisation and thus enhanced the status of the charity. Nonetheless, the image of the moneylender did not sit comfortably with the image of the charity, which in theory, relied on subscriptions and contributions for its support. Lending money was not something which a charity widely advertised but the practice was sufficiently well known to produce resentment from the general public, who were called upon to support the institutions, and for individuals to be able to apply to the charities for loans.

Such a situation arose with the Orphan Institution. A shortfall in contributions prompted the directors to inquire whether the public was under the misapprehension that the Institution was in fact quite adequately funded and not in actual need of voluntary contributions. The directors conceded the point that there were funds 'lent out on interest', the proceeds of which greatly assisted in defraying the expenses of the Institution, but protested that these funds were far from adequate. However, the annual amount of income from the interest on these bonds was not inconsiderable and for the years 1840-1842 and 1846-1850, at least, it exceeded the amount of funds that were raised by subscriptions and had by this time clearly become a guaranteed and important source of income.[41]

By 1847 the total amount of money lent on bonds by the Orphan Institution was £2,950. This represented £500 to the Town of Dundee; £700 to one John Todd's Trustees; £400 to one Duncan Robertson; £100 to one Alexander Small; £100 to one J.S. Mudie and others; and a total of £1,150, being three separate bonds, to the Dundee Harbour Trustees.[42] The Town was a regular beneficiary of financial bonds from the Dundee charitable funds, particularly in respect of projects such as the development of the new harbour. In many ways the large institutional charities were acting as conduits for the direction of community monies into community projects which may otherwise have failed to materialise - albeit without the direct knowledge of many of the contributors. The majority of contributors would have remained unaware that money loaned out in this manner not only provided security for the charitable organisations, but also contributed to the economic development of Dundee.

Challenges and change

Regardless of any such difficulties concerning the public perception of charities, organised philanthropy continued to survive in the face of challenge throughout the nineteenth century. One such challenge was the 1845 Poor Law Reform (Scotland) Act. Middle-class Scots were anxious to resist the changes of the Act. They were reluctant to lose the strong tradition of voluntary poor relief and eager to maintain local control against the threat of centralised authority. There was also a determination not to allow the charitable institutions, which were now essentially civic institutions by which many Scottish towns were recognised, to fall under the authority of an outside body. Therefore, although the Poor Law Amendment Act 'was a recognition that the voluntary principle could no longer sustain the burden of the needy', a substantial part of social welfare in Scotland did continue in the form of charitable provision.[43]

The 1845 Act empowered local parochial boards to make provision for all categories of the needy including the sick, the insane and the deaf and dumb, although existing charitable provision for these needy groups continued and expanded.[44] However, the 1845 Act also *required* the boards to provide for the pauper sick and insane.[45] Paupers who considered their pension to be inadequate were also given leave to appeal to the Board of Supervision.[46] This was contrary to the advice of the 1844 Commission which recommended that as the parochial managers would take into account the character of the pauper their decision concerning the amount of relief dispensed should be final.[47]

The response from the organised charities was that the poor law was 'at best, a necessary evil'.[48] Previously, paupers had only received a pension 'on which it was possible to live' if they were bedridden.[49] The new Act required the parochial boards to provide relief for pauper groups and to allow them the right of appeal over the relief they received, essentially contradicting everything which the charities espoused, such as the careful vetting of applicants, the moral improvement of individuals and the avoidance of their fall into pauperism. The central ethos of the organised charities founded in the early years of the nineteenth century had been the support of the deserving poor and the prevention of their descent into pauperism. The 1845 Act appeared to support the paupers in their dissipation. Furthermore, there were considerations to be made concerning the actual funding of poor relief. The Act allowed each parish the right to decide whether to raise funds for poor relief via the imposition of a poor rate or by relying on voluntary contributions.[50] However, as under the Act an assessment for the relief of the poor became an annual event after its initial implementation, this also acted as a spur to the formation and maintenance of voluntary charity in an attempt to avoid the regular implementation of a costly assessment.[51]

A further threat to the disparate urban charities came in the form of the movement towards a more integrated and co-ordinated system of philanthropy as epitomised by the Charity Organisation Society [COS]. A branch of COS was founded in Dundee in 1885. Its objects were to discourage and repress mendacity; direct the proper distribution of relief; detect imposture; prevent pauperisation resulting from indiscriminate almsgiving; and to 'systematize' the giving of charity. Annual subscribers to the charity of five shillings or more received a supply of enquiry tickets that they were urged to give to unknown beggars in lieu of money, clothes or food.[52] In a nutshell, the central aims of COS were to avoid the undeserving obtaining charity and furthermore to stop charitable monies being spent upon the demon drink.

The annual reports of COS clearly laid out its ethos, on several pages, which was perhaps necessary to inform a bemused public which up until this point had been urged to support a variety of charitable organisations and causes. The Annual Report of 1891 noted that the consequences of indiscriminate charity included street beggars. COS argued that if there was no relief there would soon be no beggars and several individual cases were described in support of their philosophy. Case number 310 concerned an unmarried, unemployed, young mother begging on the streets of Dundee. Although only 31 years old she was credited with being 'old in wickedness' and, it was claimed, would not settle at any 'honest calling.' This woman lived 'a low, drunken, immoral life' with her several illegitimate children. COS described this as a 'very bad case'.[53]

Despite their high moralising, COS appeared to have a rather naive view of the condition of the poor. The 1891 report proclaimed the Society was 'glad to be able to record a diminution during the year in the number of applications for help' which it considered reflected 'an improved condition of the working classes'.[54] This statement appeared to disregard the applications that continued to be made at the doors of the town's other charities. While 560 applications had been made to COS in 1890, the same period saw 300 applications for alms made to the Female Society and 430 to the Clothing Society, while 8,436 individuals had been helped by the Curr Night Refuge and the Children's Free Dinner had supplied 22,000 meals.[55] This was just the tip of the iceberg as far as the total amount of charitable aid in the town was concerned.

Nonetheless, while the importance of the Dundee middle classes to the foundation, support, and smooth running of the town's charities continued to be evident throughout the nineteenth century, the national trend behind active philanthropy in this period was one of social investigation, inquiry and collaboration. While COS made some rather ineffectual attempts at co-ordinating national charitable effort, a more successful strategy was that developed by the Social Union movement. The Dundee Social Union [DSU] was founded in 1888, the response of several University College professors to the poverty and misery they witnessed around them in Dundee.[56] Under the auspices of Mary Lily Walker, a resourceful and hard-working young woman who went on to found the Grey Lodge settlement house in the town, the DSU produced an influential report (1905) which attracted national attention and discussion over the terrible social conditions to be found in Dundee. The philosophy of the Social Union movement and the energy of its members ushered in a new era of social work and a greater involvement of local authorities in providing for the poorest members of society.

Notes

[1] LS, Pamphlets D5068 G, Charity Organisation Society [COS] *Annual Report* (1891).

[2] DUA, THB 1/2/2, DRI, *Annual Report* (1843); THB 1/2/1, DRI, *Annual Report* (1826).

[3] A.K. Bell, L 362.11, *Rules and Regulations of the Perth Dispensary* (1819); *Annual Report of the Perth Dispensary* (1835, 1836).

[4] LS, L.Coll. 404(1), DRI, *Annual Report* (1815).

[5] *Ibid.*

[6] O. Checkland, *Philanthropy in Victorian Scotland. Social Welfare and the Voluntary Principle* (Edinburgh, 1980), 179-180.

[7] *British Association Handbook to Dundee* (Dundee, 1912).

[8] *Report of the Home* (1849).

[9] H. Nugent, 'Poverty and Prostitution in Dundee from 1835 to 1845' (unpublished MA Dissertation, University of Dundee, 1996), 20.

[10] *Report of the Home* (1849).

[11] Nugent, 'Poverty and Prostitution', 22.

[12] *Dundee Year Book 1883.*

[13] LS, L.Coll. 53(3), cuttings re. 'The Home'.

[14] *Dundee Year Book 1883.*

[15] *Report of the Home* (1849).

[16] Checkland, *Philanthropy in Victorian Scotland*, 194-5.

[17] J. Pickstone, *Medicine and Industrial Society. A History of Hospital Development in Manchester and its Region, 1752-1946* (Manchester, 1985), 5.

[18] P. Joyce, *Work, Society and Politics. The Culture of the Factory in Later Victorian England* (London, 1980), 135.

[19] Joyce, *Work, Society and Politics*, 136.

[20] Joyce, *Work, Society and Politics,* 141.

[21] H. Blackburn, 'Baxter's Half-Time School', in Cooke, *Baxter's*, 61.

[22] M. Watson, *Jute and Flax Mills in Dundee* (Tayport, 1990), 121.

[23] W. Wilkinson, 'Housing and Health', in Cooke, *Baxter's*, 55.

[24] Watson, *Jute and Flax Mills*, 122.

[25] N. Davey notes an incident in 1846, when five female spinners from Baxter's Lower Dens works were sentenced to ten days imprisonment in the bridewell as they had left their employment without the due notice required. 'Working Conditions and Wages', in Cooke, *Baxter's*, 34.

[26] A.P. Donajgrodzki notes that social control processes could themselves be based on paternalism. Donajgrodzki (ed.), *Social Control in Nineteenth Century Britain* (London, 1977), 22.

[27] See, for example, DARC, Police Commissioners for Dundee: Register 1824-47, 24 January 1827, 78; 1838, 326.

[28] J. Myles, *Rambles in Forfarshire* (Dundee, 1850), 25, quoted in W.M. Walker, 'Irish Immigrants in Scotland: their priests, politics and parochial life', *Historical Journal*, 4 (1972), 651.

[29] DUA, THB 1/2/2, DRI, *Annual Report* (1848).

[30] Checkland, *Philanthropy*, 7.

[31] Donajgrodzki, *Social Control*, 11.

[32] R.J. Morris, 'Clubs, societies and association' in F.M.L. Thompson (ed.), *The Cambridge Social History of Britain 1750-1950, Vol.3* (Cambridge, 1993), 416.

[33] R.A. Houston, *Social Change in the Age of Enlightenment: Edinburgh, 1660-1760* Oxford, 1994), 273.

[34] F.M.L. Thompson, 'Social Control in Victorian Britain', *Economic History Review*, Vol. XXXIV (1981), 192-3.

[35] R.J. Morris and R. Roger in R.J. Morris and R. Roger (eds.), *The Victorian City. A Reader in British Urban History 1820-1914* (London, 1993), 34-35.

[36] F.K. Prochaska, 'Philanthropy' in Thompson, *Social History of Britain,* 359-60.

[37] L. Colley, *Britons. Forging the Nation 1707-1837* (London, 1992), 59.

[38] T.L. Haskell, 'Capitalism and the Origins of the Humanitarian Sensibility, Part 1', *American Historical Review,* 90 (1985). Although Haskell would possibly not agree with the suggestion that a desire to exert a form of 'social control' could form one of those preconditions.

[39] LS, L.Coll. 36(2), *An account of the Dundee Infirmary; and Report of the Committee appointed to carry into effect the proposal for a Lunatic Asylum at Dundee* (1815).

[40] StAUA, M415, Minutes Vol. 2, General Meeting, 8 June 1818.

[41] These are the only years where figures are available.

[42] DARC, GD/AY/7/1/3, DROI, Minute Book of Directors' and Special Meetings, 1830-69, Annual General Meeting, 20 October 1847

[43] Checkland, *Philanthropy*, 26.

[44] Checkland, *Philanthropy,* 324, 174, 271. Although the situation was slightly more complicated concerning care for the insane, the finance for the provisions to be made under the Lunatic Asylums (Scotland) Act (1857) came from the poor relief provisions originally made in the 1845 Act.

[45] R.A. Cage, *The Scottish Poor Law 1745-1845* (Edinburgh, 1981), 149; Checkland, *Philanthropy,* 324.

[46] Cage, *The Scottish Poor Law*, 148.

[47] Cage, *The Scottish Poor Law*, 143-4.

[48] I. Levitt, *Poverty and Welfare in Scotland 1890-1948* (Edinburgh, 1988), 15.

[49] R. Mitchison, 'The Poor Law', in Devine and Mitchison, *People and Society in Scotland Vol. 1,* 254.

[50] A. Paterson, 'The poor law in nineteenth-century Scotland', in D. Fraser (ed.), *The New Poor Law in the Nineteenth Century* (London, 1976), 175.

[51] Cage, *The Scottish Poor Law*, 147.

[52] LS, Pamphlets, D5068 G, COS, *Annual Report* (1891).

[53] *Ibid.*

[54] *Ibid.*

[55] *Dundee Year Book 1891.*

[56] Schafe, *University Education in Dundee*, 19.

Conclusion

Image and Identity

'Never have benevolent, philanthropic, and social and sanitary reforming movements been more active.'[1]

The development of organised charity was part of a larger and more complex picture than can be explained by religious humanitarianism, a desire to control the industrial working classes or simply meeting the basic needs of the poor. The 'needs' of the Dundee middle classes, in terms of their desire to advance themselves both as individuals and as a group, were reflected in the use of organised charity as a vehicle to express civic pride in addition to consolidating their influence in the town. The Victorian philanthropists' holistic view of life has been described as one which did not distinguish between religious and social welfare, but considered them as one and the same.[2] This view can also be extended to include the welfare of the civic, social and economic community in which the philanthropists were both living and at the same time creating. The ability to simultaneously deal with aspects of urban poverty, to promote the civic standing of Dundee and advance the position of the town's middle-class elite were seen as compatible activities.

The opportunity to achieve this was facilitated by the urban middle-class propensity for establishing and participating in a wide range of voluntary associations. Scotland's tradition of voluntary poor relief in many ways laid the foundation for the development of a system of organised charity. However, this did not necessarily facilitate the widespread acceptance of such a development. Dundee did not establish as wide a range of charitable institutions as the other major Scottish towns of the period and failed to establish certain charitable institutional forms, particularly a lying-in facility, a Lock hospital and a Magdalene asylum. While it is unlikely that the provision of these institutions would have radically altered the condition of the town's poor what was more important were the philosophy and aims which lay behind the activities of the urban philanthropists, not only in their decisions to develop certain charities but also in their resolve not to countenance the establishment of others.[3] The charitable organisations established and supported by Dundee's middle class, both men and women, demonstrated the way in which they wanted their community to develop.

One of the main reasons for the lack of support given to the organised charities was their class-specific nature. The continuing development of a class-based society throughout the nineteenth century necessarily implied a movement towards group-specific ideologies and a movement away from community-specific interests.[4] While many of the organised charities appeared to involve the whole community in terms of the upper, middle and working classes as either patrons, organisers or recipients, the idea of inter-class sympathy or a drawing together of the classes through these forms of contact was largely illusory. Charitable societies were organisations whose interests were always articulated in terms of class, and specifically the interests of those who were most closely involved with the organisational and financial structure of these institutions - the middle classes.

Furthermore, many aspects of the development of the charitable organisations appears to have made many townspeople somewhat sceptical of their benefits and uses, particularly the way in which the funds were handled in relation to the development of the charity, the involvement of business and when civic or personal conflict in the running of the organisations occurred. This scepticism was perhaps best exemplified in the initial enthusiasm with which original subscriptions were raised for the establishment of a charity, followed by the constant struggle which the majority of the organisations then faced in maintaining long-term practical viability. It may also explain the resentment and hostility which many of the charities experienced.

The subjective element of philanthropic activity is, of course, impossible to ascertain. In the majority of cases, however, the constraints appear to have been more persuasive than the positive influences. The Dundee Infirmary alone out of the charitable organisations established in the period could boast a relatively widespread support while many others struggled constantly to maintain a financial and practical viability. The monies which the individual philanthropists made available in the form of charitable gestures; the funds the organised societies provided in the form of loans to the Town and its projects; and the support which was withheld from the establishment of charitable organisations enjoyed by other Scottish towns, were all central to the development of nineteenth-century Dundee.

Notes

[1] *Dundee Year Book 1879.*

[2] F.K. Prochaska, *The Voluntary Impulse. Philanthropy in Modern Britain* (London, 1988), xiii.

[3] Checkland, *Philanthropy*, 240-1.

[4] For a discussion of this idea see P. Hills, 'Division and cohesion in the nineteenth-century middle class: the case of Ipswich 1830-1870', *Urban History Yearbook* (1987), 42-50.